Kornelia Freitag (Ed.)

Apocalypse Soon?

masteRResearch

herausgegeben von / edited by

Walter Grünzweig, Randi Gunzenhäuser,
Sibylle Klemm, Sina Nitzsche, Julia Sattler

Band / Volume 3

LIT

Apocalypse Soon?

Religion and Popular Culture
in the United States

edited by

Kornelia Freitag

LIT

Cover Picture: Pierre Hattwig and Heike Steinhoff

Bibliographic information published by the Deutsche Nationalbibliothek
The Deutsche Nationalbibliothek lists this publication in the Deutsche
Nationalbibliografie; detailed bibliographic data are available in the Internet at
http://dnb.d-nb.de.

ISBN 978-3-643-90117-0

A catalogue record for this book is available from the British Library

©LIT VERLAG GmbH & Co. KG Wien,
Zweigniederlassung Zürich 2011
Klosbachstr. 107
CH-8032 Zürich
Tel. +41 (0) 44-251 75 05
Fax +41 (0) 44-251 75 06
e-Mail: zuerich@lit-verlag.ch
http://www.lit-verlag.ch

LIT VERLAG Dr. W. Hopf
Berlin 2011
Fresnostr. 2
D-48159 Münster
Tel. +49 (0) 2 51-620 320
Fax +49 (0) 2 51-23 19 72
e-Mail: lit@lit-verlag.de
http://www.lit-verlag.de

Distribution:
In Germany: LIT Verlag Fresnostr. 2, D-48159 Münster
Tel. +49 (0) 2 51-620 32 22, Fax +49 (0) 2 51-922 60 99, e-mail: vertrieb@lit-verlag.de

In Austria: Medienlogistik Pichler-ÖBZ, e-mail: mlo@medien-logistik.at
In the UK: Global Book Marketing, e-mail: mo@centralbooks.com

Contents

Contents

Introduction

IN GOD WE TRUST: Religion and Culture in the United States

KORNELIA FREITAG

Take a dollar bill, flip it over, and look at the line directly above the central image: "IN GOD WE TRUST" is displayed in capital letters under the name of the country. This motto is as good a reminder as any other that religion is deeply engrained in the life of the United States. This is and has been true for the country's everyday life as much as for its politics and its media. Religion has played a part in settling the North American continent, in founding the United States, and in shaping its self-image as well as its idea of the rest of the world. It is a part of political rhetoric and a source for popular culture, from Bob Dylan's 1960s outright critical "With God on Our Side," which has never gone out of fashion and experienced a renewed revival after the country's reaction to 9/11; to Madonna's ambiguous 1988 pop video "Like a Prayer," which sent Christians on both sides of the Atlantic rallying and Coca Cola to cut her advertising contract (Hulsether); and to Mel Gibson's devout 2004 blockbuster *The Passion of the Christ*, which was much praised, debunked, and pirated (Marez). Religion is, in short, pervasive in daily life.

In the first chapter of their 2008 analysis of religion in contemporary U.S. politics, David Domke and Kevin Coe observe that, unlike any other industrially developed country, "America is a place where one's beliefs about God are a significant component of daily life" (11). Based on a mass of survey data drawn from Gallup, National Election Studies, and the General Social Survey, they substantiate this insight and write that

large majorities of American adults have integrated elements of faith into their daily experiences. On a constant basis, roughly 70% say they pray several times a week or more, and about 60% claim that faith provides a "great deal" or "quite a bit" of guidance in their day-to-day lives. Similar results can be found in the confidence of U.S. adults about their religious beliefs: nearly 90% consistently say "I never doubt the existence of God," and slightly more than 80% consistently say that people will be called before God on a judgement day. (11-12)

The authors conclude, what was already shown in the country's popular culture and its paper money: "faith runs wide and deep in America" (12).

R. Marie Griffith and Melani McAlister, the editors of a special issue of the *American Quarterly* on "Religion and Politics in the Contemporary United States," start from a completely opposite vantage point when they write that

3

commentators across the political spectrum have expressed increasingly outspoken concerns about the "marginalization" of faith. From Joseph Lieberman to Barack Obama, from liberal evangelicals to mainstream Muslims, politicians and observers have decried the lack of attention to religion, and lack of respect for religious people, in U.S. politics. Not for the first time in U.S. history, there is a profound sense of crisis about the unsettled relationship between religion and politics in our public life. (528)

Yet, on second glance, the "concerns about the 'marginalization' of faith" that the editors find rippling from left to right (which is given extensive room at the beginning of the article) and across denominational divides, are in themselves good proof of Domke's and Coe's point about religion's central role – one would not really complain about the "marginalization" of something that was already, well, marginalized.

Does this mean that in the U.S. religion "rules"? This would be a crass oversimplification. In fact, since its very foundation there have been laws in place that forbid state entities in the U.S. to interfere with anyone's faith or to establish a state religion. It is absolutely unimaginable for U.S. citizens that the state might inquire about their faith on tax forms, even less that it would oversee the payment of taxes to specific denominations. In a way, the general understanding is that religion is everybody's own and very private business, while an overwhelming majority of U.S. citizens is convinced that religious faith – their faith or any faith, there the opinions part – is the basis for a moral life, for the individual and the nation. In the 1960s, sociologist Robert N. Bellah termed this faith-based national ethos, the outcome of the "common elements of religious orientation that the great majority of Americans share," "American civil religion." His observation that this basic religious orientation has "played a crucial role in the development of American institutions and still provide[s] a religious dimension for the whole fabric of American life, including the political sphere" (171) holds still true today – and is the explanation for the very intimate and effective relationship between religion and popular culture discussed in many of the following essays.

While the historical development in the U.S. ensured the special interrelation of religion and society in the U. S., this has never meant a clear-cut or stable relationship between the two. What Domke and Coe concentrate on and criticize in their study of state politics regarding election campaigns over the last three decades is the astonishing return of overt Christianity-grounded strategies after their previous ebbing. The *American Quarterly* special issue provides an even broader look at the changes in the contemporary state of U.S. political-religious affairs. To the editors, the "profound sense of crisis about the unsettled relationship between religion and politics in our public life" currently perceived on all sides in the U.S. (and investigated from one angle by Domke and Coe) "conspicuously quickened after September 11, 2001." One religion, Islam, started to be "repeatedly vilified;" and a sharp distinction was drawn between "'good' religion, which seemed calm, rational, and moderate in its claims on public life" – in other words, 'our' Western-tradition religion (read: 'Christianity')

– and "'dangerous' religion, which is to say any form of Islam that positioned itself or its adherents as 'anti-American'" (528). This puts a distinctly new spin on earlier arguments that religion had "not only [...] a role in politics; [but was] at the heart of the enterprise" (527), or – with Bellah – on "American civil religion."

Another point the editors make concerns the composition of religious beliefs in the U.S. and, in particular, its diversification over the last four decades and a half. They supply data drawn from the 2001 American Religious Identification Survey (ARIS) carried out by the City University of New York that show that the religious make-up of the United States is changing slowly but steadily. They argue convincingly that this was caused in particular by the Immigration and Naturalization Services Act of 1965, which abandoned the severe restrictions on immigration from Latin America, Asia, Africa, and the Middle East:

The percentage of Protestant Christians has dropped from 64.3 to 50.4 percent of the population since 1974, while the percentage of Catholics has remained steady at about 25 percent. [...] The total percentage of Jews, Muslims, Buddhists, Hindus, and others is still relatively small, between 5 percent and 8 percent of the population, but that is a substantive increase from 0.5 percent in 1974. (Griffith and McAllister 540-541)

Apart from this, the editors also point towards the importance of the rising internal diversification of denominations and movements of new spiritualities (541) as well as "the increasing focus among religious believers upon transnationalism and diversity" (540).

This is, of course, a fascinating field for scholars and students of U.S. culture and history, who want to go beyond stating the obvious and ask what the cultural function of religion and faith(s) might be and formerly have been; how and in what ways (and guises) religion has or has not influenced public life; and how the general social and media development has impacted and is still impacting religious forms of expression. As these and many further questions have by no means been answered yet, the 2007 annual convention of the German Association of American Studies on "Religion in the U.S.A." at Bochum and Dortmund drew not only an unusually large crowd of scholars and critics from all over the world (cf. Cortiel et al.) but also raised great attention among the students living and studying in the area.

A graduate seminar at Ruhr-University Bochum resulted in a whole array of perceptive papers which were presented and intensely scrutinized in a workshop that followed the conference. As the papers were overall much more engaging and intensely researched than 'normal' seminar work, the students in the group decided to put together a publication. The result of this effort, which took much longer than anticipated but has thereby definitely gained in depth, is the current collection.

The seminar had been structured to benefit from the input by the many experts at the conference while the students, at the same time, were totally free to choose any subject related to "Religion in the U.S.A." that they wished. Thus, it may come as a little surprise that almost all of them took their cues from the investigations of U.S. culture by Paul S. Boyer and Heather Hendershot, the latter being especially influential with her focus on media studies. Although other possibilities would have been available, the two scholars' combination of a historically informed critique of evangelicalism and fundamentalism with the critical analysis of their current cultural effects seems definitely to have hit a nerve.

Hence, seven of the nine essays in this collection perform close readings of a variety of texts representing popular culture, from music to TV shows to internet pages advertising Christian diet and chastity programs, while two are devoted to millennialism and apocalyptic thought in the history and politics of the U.S.A. respectively. As a consequence, history and politics are underrepresented, although they have been especially important in shaping the specific nexus of religion and culture described above. Hence, I will sketch out on the remaining pages of this introduction the historical and political history of the dominant religious discourse in the United States before I introduce the essays that are collected herein.

"A Citty Upon a Hill"

Unquestionably, even before the very birth of the nation, religion had a significant role in founding a number of the colonies that would later be in the forefront of forming "a more perfect union." None of the texts from the Puritans' bible-based "stream of rhetorical self-definition" (Berkovitch 34) is better known than the sermon "A Modell of Christian Charity" that John Winthrop preached in 1630 to almost 400 fellow emigrants aboard the Arbella, which took them to America:

For wee must consider that wee shall be as a citty upon a hill. The eies of all people are uppon us. Soe that if wee shall deale falsely with our God in this worke wee haue undertaken, and soe cause him to withdrawe his present help from us, wee shall be made a story and a by-word through the world. Wee shall open the mouthes of our enemies to speake evill of the wayes of God, and all professors for God's sake. Wee shall shame the faces of many of God's worthy servants, and cause theire prayers to be turned into curses upon us till we be consumed out of the good land whither we are going. (47)

In no uncertain terms the sermon frames the experience of the settlers, whose first governor Winthrop was to become, as an act of biblical proportions. It shows the Puritans as "a community that invented its identity *ex verbo,* by the word, and continued to assert this identity through the seventeenth century" (Berkovitch ibid.). Timothy Goering's essay, the first in the volume, clarifies some of the reasons for their bible-steeped world view.

The Puritans were radical in promoting their faith and especially prolific in preserving it in print, and thus they came to hold a special place in the history and the literature of the American colonies and the United States. Winthrop's sermon is one of the key texts of American historiography and became "enshrined as a kind of Ur-text of American literature" (Delbanco 72). Yet also in the non-Puritan colonies and after the demise of the Puritan world view, Protestant Christianity would dominate the intellectual and political climate in the part of North America that was to become the United States. Although it was never the only belief system – and was internally divided in many, often bitterly warring sects and factions – at least until World War II, it easily pushed aside and obliterated native spirituality, Catholicism, or other beliefs brought by immigrants from all over the world.

Thus the rebellion of the colonies against the British Crown was put on a thoroughly Christian basis already by the very formulation in the Declaration of Independence that justified the American colonists' entitlement to "dissolve the bands" with Britain with "the laws of nature and of nature's God" and argued that the self-evident truth "that all men are created equal," rested on being "endowed by their Creator with certain unalienable Rights" (Bellah 173-174, Guétin 30-45). And thus it is only logical that God would also be summoned when the first government of the new state was formed. As Domke and Coe put it:

Religion formally entered the U.S. presidency at its inception, when George Washington, in his 1789 inaugural address, declared that "it would be peculiarly improper to omit in this first official act my fervent supplications to that Almighty Being who rules over the universe." (6)

Yet while this formulation would not have raised even one eyebrow among his listeners and while it is quoted as one of the founding documents of "civil religion" by Bellah (174), there were some Founding Fathers (notably Jefferson and Madison) who were concerned about the possibly detrimental effects of the establishment of one creed as a state religion. The separation of church and state became one of the big issues in drafting and ratifying the Constitution – and one of the important principles in "American civil religion."

The problem was solved – for the time being – by the Founding Fathers' addition of the First Amendment to the Constitution. It assures freedom of expression and demands congress to "make no law respecting an establishment of religion." Yet one might also read the amendment on the freedom of religion, speech, press, and assembly less as the solution to than as the acknowledgement of a set of troubling problems that were not solved in the main text. In the more positive terms of communication theorist and historian James Carey, the amendment secures the establishment of a "compact way of describing a political society [...] an attempt to define the nature of public life" (216-217). But, he also stresses that "[o]f all the freedoms of public life in

7

the eighteenth century, freedom of religion was, perhaps, the most difficult liberty for Americans to adjust to" (217).

While it is still the dominant popular opinion that the separation of church and state was established by the first Amendment in the Bill of Rights, discussion of this assumption has been spurred again, at least since Ronald Reagan took office (Domke and Coe, Hall, Griffith and McAlister). The astonishing mingling of religious and public spheres has lasted well into George Bush's two terms in the White House and it has clearly influenced the last election campaign, in which not only the Republicans but also both Democratic candidates, Hillary Clinton and Barack Obama "felt the need to address the general religious sentiment" (Cortiel et al. 9). As David D. Hall has argued in his discussion of the renewed debates of the relationship between "Church and State" (105-110), when "activists and historians" from both sides of the political spectrum, as well as Christian fundamentalists and evangelicals started

to reflect anew on the question of what the Founders had intended with the First Amendment clauses on religion [,] [...] polemicists on each side have busied themselves ransacking the historical record, one side extracting statements that make the Founders sound like conventional Christians, the other, reconstructing the anxieties of a Jefferson and Madison (and many others) about the future of the new republic were it to accept any form of state-affiliated Christianity. (108)

He goes on to quote historian Richard Wilson's observation that the Founders did not suggest the "wholesale segregation [of religion] from government—the kind of resolution proposed in the French Revolution—for separationist logic opens the way for radical secularization as a social policy" (Hall 109).

Roughly three and a half decades after the signing of the Constitution and the Bill of Rights, Alexis de Tocqueville, the famous French traveller and observer of American democracy still stressed that it was "the religious aspect of the country that first struck [his] eye" (282) on his arrival. Yet he praised what amounts to the successful moderation of the relationship between religion and the state by the First Amendment when he describes America as

the place in the world where the Christian religion has most preserved genuine powers over souls; and nothing shows better how useful and natural to man it is in our day, since the country in which it exercises the greatest empire is at the same time the most enlightened and the most free. (278)

Much might be said – and has been said – about this very optimistic rendering of the relationship between U.S. democracy and Christianity at the end of the first third of the 19th century. Not even all Christians were "free" in the same way as, for instance, Philip Hamburger's argument shows that the famous principle of the separation of church and state was, among other things, an effective means to keep Catholics from winning influence in public life (Hall 109). One might also note that in the whole history of the U.S. presidency up to today, only one Catholic, John F. Kennedy, has ever managed to be elected, although Catholics have always formed an important part of the total U.S. population.

In his election campaign Kennedy insisted that he "believe[d] in an America where the separation of church and state is absolute; where no Catholic prelate would tell the President – should he be Catholic – how to act, and no Protestant minister would tell his parishioners for whom to vote" (qtd. in Domke and Coe 6). That Kennedy had to stress this in a campaign speech in 1960 shows that although the First Amendment may well argue for and secure a separation between church and state, this separation could by no means always be taken for granted. And, as Domke and Coe are quick to point out, Kennedy's argument "was a welcome message then; it would be almost unimaginable today" (6), that is in 2008.

But before we can turn to our own time in this overview on some of the especially important milestones in the ways in which (Christian) religion has been inscribed into U.S. state history and "American civil religion" was shaped, at least one further faith-based 19th century discourse needs to be mentioned: the idea of America's "Manifest Destiny" (also Guétin 65-80). It underpinned the expansion of U.S. territory throughout the 19th century and was formulated by the journalist John L. O'Sullivan in 1845. After he coined the term in the summer of that year, in order to justify the annexation of Texas, he used it in a famous lead editorial in the *New York Morning News* on 27 December 1845, where he claimed that the right of the U.S. to all of Oregon rested on

the right of our manifest destiny to overspread and to possess the whole of the continent which Providence has given for the development of the great experiment of liberty and federative self-government entrusted to us. It is a right such as that of the tree to the space of air and earth suitable for the full expansion of its principle and destiny of growth. (qtd. in Sampson 200)

The phrase "manifest destiny" and the concept behind it would, henceforth, become one of the pillars of U.S. foreign politics. Put into a nutshell, it starts from the same idea that Winthrop had used to prepare his fellow emigrants for crossing the Atlantic and settling "the good land whither [they were] going" – namely, that land acquisition was preordained and sacred by God: "Providence" is still the basis for O'Sullivan's "manifest destiny," only that the aim is no longer to add to God's glory by erecting "a citty upon a hill," but to spread democracy for its own sake, i.e. "the great experiment of liberty and federated self-government" which, as implicitly the argument still is, God had "entrusted to us."

It is easy to see how the still loosely faith-based 19th century claim to a "manifest destiny" could – with time – become more or less cut off from its original religious justification, how it could be of use in a more secular environment. Whether with explicit or latent religious underpinnings, it came to justify any kind of regional or global

9

interference, annexation, or expansion in the name of spreading democracy outside the original borders of the U.S.: in the remainder of North America (including islands inside and outside of the hemisphere), South America, Indochina, or Iraq. The ideology of an explicitly religious manifest destiny-politics "With God on Our side" has been criticized time and again. Bob Dylan's 1960s anti-war song condemns it. Even Bellah argues in his article that civil religion was "not the worship of the American nation but an understanding of the American experience in the light of ultimate and universal reality" (186). Yet, the concept of manifest destiny remains starkly outlined in his characterization of "American civil religion" as "concerned that America be a society as perfectly in accord with the will of God as men can make it, and a light to all nations" (ibid.).

Given the tradition of an American civil religion, and its ambiguity, it is not too surprising that after a time of a relative decline of religious justification in U.S. politics since the 1960s, in the 1980s religiosity in U.S. government politics could gain new strength. "Religion," argue Domke and Coe,

is now a defining fault line, with citizens' religious affinities, regularity of worship, and perception of "moral values" among the strongest predictors of presidential voting patterns. Political leaders have taken advantage of and contributed to the developments through calculated, deliberate, and partisan use of faith. We call this the *God Strategy*. (7)

This argument takes us to the ways in which religion is used in the contemporary scene – which provides a direct link to Raphaela Holinski's investigation of George W. Bush's use of religion in foreign policy in the second essay of this collection. Finished well before the publication of Domke's and Coe's book and therefore not using the term, her contribution, nonetheless, fleshes out the *God Strategy* in a number of keen observations on the 43rd President's speeches, also contextualizing them in the particular brand of evangelicalism he favored.

The Essays

In the first essay of this volume, "The New World, the Old World, and the End of It," Daniel Timothy Goering starts his discussion of Puritan apocalyptic thinking with observations on how systems of thought and language predetermine the expression of cultural and political fears. Arguing that "[o]ur culture is no less apocalyptic than any other – but in fact has an entirely new apocalyptic language and system," he calls for a serious treatment of earlier (and different) world views (from our own) that should not be quickly written off as superstition or rhetoric but instead seriously studied and put into perspective. Thus he prepares us for his take on the Puritan ideas about the end of the world. Drawing on Perry Miller and Avihu Zakai, he argues that the Puritans' powerful apocalyptic system was more than rhetoric but rested on "two main axes:

sacralized time and sacralized space" that allowed them "to give meaning and purpose to their migration to New England."

Raphaela Holinski's contribution to the volume continues the discussion of an apocalyptic world view yet turns towards our own time by inspecting "The World Caught Between *Good* and *Evil*: Elements of Evangelicalism in U.S. Foreign Policy." Her central question is "how the evangelical body of thought and in particular the element of prophecy belief can be found in President George W. Bush's speeches on foreign policy." To answer this question she starts by characterizing basic premises of evangelicalism and its currently most popular strand, premillennial dispensationalism, before she engages in close readings of a number of speeches, addresses, and talks of the 43rd President of the United States of America. She concludes that "Bush's understanding of America's mission (the old idea of 'manifest destiny') is not identical to" the premillennialists' view of the world. Yet, as she demonstrates in her essay, he was still able to persuade them to endorse his politics by the adoption of a "Manichean moral code" and the use of "a religious frame of reference which lends itself to the premillennialists' self-perception as those who carry out God's will and are part of His divine plan."

The subsequent five essays are devoted to various ways in which U.S. popular culture and religion interact. Two deal with rock music, three with TV-series. The first, Moritz Schuster's discussion of a rock star's take on the apocalypse, "Marilyn Manson – the All-American Antichrist? Prophecy Belief in U.S. Pop Culture," analyses Manson's manipulation of religious sentiments in his "band construct," more specifically, how "he constructs his persona as the Antichrist," how "his frequent use of Christian elements [...] makes it easy for most U.S. people to relate to his lyrics," and, finally, how "he offers his fans a substitute for or antidote to traditional religion." His discussion of the star's extreme modes of self-fashioning and his readings of key texts show how – over time and with growing success – the antichrist-stance is strategically modified in order to accommodate the public taste, while "Marilyn Manson's references to Biblical imagery have remained an important basis for his lasting success."

In "The Style/Content Dissonance: The Use of Popular Culture in Evangelical Music," Cornelius Herz turns to a totally opposite sphere from Manson's, namely the evangelical music market. Yet, of course, with the idea of the "Saviour" the apocalypse is still central to Saviour Machine's lyrics and also the analysis of the "band construct" (Schuster) of the group shows quite an important overlap with "secular" Gothic groups. Starting from the observation of a "style/content dissonance" in evangelical music by Heather Hendershot, Herz follows the contradiction between "music with a content that can be classified as evangelical and a style that can be classified as secular" and comes to the conclusion "that it is especially the interaction with secular music" that allows a band like Saviour Machine "to create and relate their own identity beyond the religious and the secular, somewhere in-between."

While the apocalypse is pretty much out of the picture in Gunnar Berndt's "Reaching out to the Masses: An Analysis of the Evangelical Television Series *Family First*," religious ambiguities and ties to the secular world abound in the sitcom/drama *Family First*. He argues that the show is thinly veiled propaganda against the "three central sins as identified by Christian fundamentalism – namely pre-marital sex, homosexuality, and abortion," yet does not use openly bible-based arguments but "hides its religious aims under a secular [and emotionalized] plot and thereby sends only ambiguously religious messages." Drawing on various media critics he concludes that by tuning down overtly religious messages and by boosting emotional ones, the makers of the show react to both changed modes of perception in the "Age of Television" and pursue a strategy of reaching out across the borders of the evangelical community to the wider public: "What appears to have become of sole importance is *that* certain religious values prevail in the general population. That they prevail *for religious reasons* appears almost entirely insignificant."

The next two essays are devoted to TV-productions that leave the evangelical realm. But, as both Christian Lenz's "'Death Becomes Her': Representations of Death, Afterlife and God in American TV-Series" and Maria Verena Siebert's "Religion in *Lost*: Managing a National Crisis on U.S. Television" demonstrate, religious connotations, plot lines, imagery, and ideologies are mainstays of popular entertainment. In his analysis, which is mainly devoted to the TV-series *Dead Like Me*, Lenz explores "the notions and connections of death, the afterlife and the function of God with respect to them" in parts of contemporary mainstream television. His discussion of the series' irreverent rendering of death – the reasons and ways of dying and death's popular personification of Grim Reaper's fame – as well as of the structure of the (not so) sweet thereafter leads him to the conclusion that "the series strikingly suggests that god has become a mere Baudrillardian simulacrum of the third order" and "that although 'God' and 'death' are still in usage as Christian signifiers, it is the latter which keeps its power up to now whereas the former needn't be filled with any meaning anymore."

Contrary to the thoroughly secular message in *Dead Like Me*, Siebert's reading of one of the most popular post-9/11 TV-series reveals strong, if carefully hidden, religious undertones to anchor its plot. Moving from explicit towards implicit layers of religious discourse in the mystery-drama *Lost,* she proves that while in isolated episodes Catholicism is overtly used (and, as so often, othered) to bolster the underlying message of faith and righteousness as a means of crisis management, the whole show uses in various hidden ways American civil religion for spreading a nationalist message. In her close readings she unmistakably demonstrates *Lost* to be "a conservative reaction to the crisis of 9/11 that helps code a secular national catastrophe in terms of a quasi-religious test for the chosen American people."

The last two essays in the collection are devoted to religion as a technique that targets in particular girls and young women and aims at shaping and controlling the body and bodily drives. Petra Danielczyk traces in "The Link between Eating Disorders and Religion: Re-encoding the Urge for Thinness" the background, effects, and dangers of the "Weigh Down" program of the Christian fundamentalist Gwen Shamblin. Starting from the question, "why do Christian fundamentalists turn to dieting and in its course to eating disorders?" Danielczyk scrutinizes from a cultural studies perspective the publications of Shamblin, of followers who praise the program's success, and of drop-outs who talk about its damage. She points out that the danger of re-coding a bodily illness into a religious obligation lies in the explanatory logic in which "failure is at-tributed to the individual while success is attributed to God." In both cases the major reasons for eating disorders – "the lack of feeling self-worth and the general lack of control" – are not addressed. They are, in fact, even reinforced. Hence, Danielczyk concludes, "a shallow re-coding of thinness from worldly to religious concern runs the risk to lead into other addictions or mental illnesses."

With "Identity, Morals, and Visibility: The Virginity Pledge Movement and Popu-lar Culture" Elisa Edwards addresses a closely related issue, namely, another way to regulate identity construction – here via the pledge to abstain from sexual activity in the name of Christian morality. By drawing upon many concrete examples from the web pages of the movement "The Silver Ring Thing," she demonstrates in pointed analyses "how this 'identity movement' and 'moral community' functions through the use of popular culture, the ascription of specific moral values, the representation of nonpledgers as 'the others,' and the suggestion of specific gender roles." Compara-ble to Danielczyk, Herz, and Berndt, Edwards shows the embedding of the religious movement in popular and consumer culture. At the end of her essay she points out that "[b]etween 1996 and 2006 alone, Congress and state governments spent \$1.5 billion to support abstinence organizations." By hinting at the ongoing controversy concern-ing the relationship between church and state (Domke and Coe, Hall, Griffith and McAllister), she suggests that "it would be interesting to have a closer look at these veiled interconnections between state and religious movement in a country which prides itself in its complete division between church and state."

The seminar and the work on the essays proved to be an eye-opening, sometimes harrowing, at other times enlightening experience for all participants. With our sincere thanks to Evangelia Kindinger, Aischa Konaté, and Elisa and Jason Edwards, who put much thought and effort to revising and finishing the manuscript. Thanks also to Brian Reed, who was supportive as ever. We now offer the volume to the readers of the masteRResearch series in the hope that some of our collective insight will come across.

Works Cited

Bellah, Robert N. *Beyond Belief: Essays on Religion in a Post-Traditionalist World*. Berkeley: U of California P, 1991. 168-86. Print.

Berkovitch, Sacvan. "The Puritan Vision of New England." *Columbia Literary History of the United States*. Ed. Emory Elliott. New York: Columbia UP, 1988. 33-44. Print.

Carey, James. "'A Republic, I You Can Keep It': Liberty and Public Life in the Age of Glasnost." *James Carey: A Critical Reader*. Eds. Eve Stryker Munson and Catherine A. Warren. Minneapolis: U of Minnesota P, 1997. 207-27. Print.

Cortiel, Jeanne, Kornelia Freitag, Christine Gerhardt and Michael Wala, eds. *Religion in the United States*. Heidelberg: Winter, 2010. Print.

Delbanco, Andrew. *The Puritan Ideal*. Cambridge, Mass.: Harvard UP, 1989. Print.

Domke, David and Kevin Coe. *The God Strategy: How Religion became a Political Weapon in America*. Oxford, New York: Oxford UP, 2008. Print.

Griffith, R. Marie, and Melani McAlister. "Introduction: Is the Public Square Still Naked?" *American Quarterly Special Issue: Religion and Politics in the Contemporary United States* 3 (Sept 2007): 527-63. Print.

Guétin, Nicole. *Religious Ideology in American Politics: A History*. Jefferson: McFarland, 2009. Print.

Hall, David. "The Present and the Past in the Religious History of the United States." *Religion in the United States*. Eds. Jeanne Cortiel et al. Heidelberg: Winter, 2010. 99-116. Print.

Hamburger, Philip. *Separation of Church and State: A Theologically Liberal, Anti-Catholic, and American Principle*. Chicago: U of Chicago P, 2002. Print.

Hulsether, Mark D. "Like a Sermon: Popular Religion in Madonna Videos." *Religion and Popular Culture in America*. 2nd rev. ed. Eds. Bruce David Forbes and Jeffrey H. Mahan. Berkeley: U of California P, 2005. 75-98. Print.

Marez, Curtis. Preface. *American Quarterly Special Issue: Religion and Politics in the Contemporary United States* 3 (Sept 2007): vii-ix. Print.

Sampson, Robert D. *John O'Sullivan and His Times*. Kent: Kent State UP, 2003. Print.

Tocqueville, Alexis de. *Democracy in America*. Ed. and trans. Harvey C. Mansfield and Delba Winthrop. Chicago: U of Chicago P, 2000. Print.

Winthrop, John. "A Modell of Christian Charity." *Massachusetts Historical Society Collections*. 3rd series vol. VII. Boston: Charles Little and James Brown, 1838. 33-48. Print.

Millennialism and Apocalypse

The Old World, the New World, and the End of It

Daniel Timothy Goering

I would like to begin this paper with a short reference to an occurrence in the Middle Ages. It enfolded in the year 1064, which was a special year because it was going to lure many thousands from their homes on a pilgrimage towards Jerusalem (Möhring 27). Why? Because the calendar had something extraordinary to offer. The astonishing coincidence was that in the year 1064 Easter fell on 27 March. This information alone was capable of thrusting many thousands into an apocalyptic haze. The question, as to why this information had such an impact, would have been simply answered by the pilgrim of 1064: "If Easter is on 27 March then that means Good Friday (the day on which Jesus was crucified) would be celebrated on Friday 25 March!" A second inquiry as to why this was astonishing would have then been explained by the pilgrim: "Because 25 March is obviously Annunciation Day!" This is the day when Mary, the mother of Jesus, was told that she was pregnant with the Son of God. Therefore, if 25 March is Annunciation Day and simultaneously Good Friday, then – symbolically speaking – *in the year 1064 Jesus was conceived and died on the same day*. History, thus, had been completed and had been brought to fruition – the world was ready to take its leave. In the midst of this 'evidence' it was self-explanatory to many medieval Christians that Jesus would have to return a second time for the final judgment on Easter 1064. In the minds of medieval Christians it was obvious that the place where the world would "groan" (Romans 8,23) one last time would be Jerusalem. Thus, many thousands left everything behind and decided to go and praise the coming King at Jerusalem. They embarked on a journey that would not lead to salvation but rather to their death. Almost all of the pilgrims died either on their journey to Jerusalem or on their way back, after experiencing the sobering disappointment that the world had not come to an end (Möhring).

The questions we as students of Cultural Studies must ask include: why did this coincidence in the calender have such an effect in 1064? Why can we not relate to the reaction of so many thousands? Why does the fact that Good Friday might fall on the same day as Annunciation Day not put us into a delirious frenzy in modern times, as it did to so many in 1064? What separates us from them? The simple but very scanty answer is: 1000 years ago a different cultural and apocalyptic language was spoken. That is, the calendar had an utterly different meaning than it has now and the cyclical conception vis-à-vis the later linear conception of history was prevalent in the apocalyptic mindset.

I started with this example because I would like to sensitize our attention to the power of apocalyptic systems and apocalyptic language. The reason we do not have the desire to rush to Jerusalem once we hear that Good Friday might happen to fall on Annunciation Day is not that we are 'enlightened,' or supposedly secularized, or that we 'know better,' but that we are deaf to that particular apocalyptic language. We speak a different language. One that reeks of 'scientific analyses' and self proclaimed 'experts' who have a seemingly divine gift for calculating how soon we would be able to destroy this world single-handedly, if we do not begin throwing away our plastic cups into the correct plastic containers. The scientists and anchormen of our day do not work for 'non-prophet organizations' – they are excessively prophetic. No one who attentively listens to the daily news could miss the modern dogma that our existence in this frail world is in fact, finally, coming to a close. The language with which this is described is compounded of acronyms such as Y2K, BSE or CO_2, or concepts such as 'global warming' and 'climate change,' which could only make the pilgrim of 1064 sarcastically chuckle at our folly. Our culture is no less apocalyptic than any other – but in fact has an entirely new apocalyptic language and system that is set apart from previous apocalyptic languages and systems in dramatic ways.

It is also important to note that apocalyptic systems are not solely rhetorical. The modern apocalyptic language only works because it refers to our modern apocalyptic system: one that is framed by a triumvirate of *ratio*, science and media. The words do not contain power intrinsically; rather they are the ammunition which could only become 'lethal' if utilized with the correct weapon. In sum, the power of apocalyptic systems lies not solely in the apocalyptic rhetoric, but rather in the encrypted mindset which rhetoric is capable of activating and unlocking.

One specific apocalyptic system that is important for an understanding of the impact of apocalyptic thought in the U.S. public sphere today is that of the Puritans of the 17th century. Puritans believed themselves to be the chosen ones who would watch how the world would crumble and fall before their eyes. It is evident that they employed apocalyptic rhetoric with great vehemence, but I would like to move beyond this rhetoric. An analysis that rests only on apocalyptic rhetoric will always remain unsatisfying, because it provides only half the picture. I would prefer to analyze the system by asking: why did this language work? How did the apocalyptic system function? *What is the anatomy of the apocalyptic system in Puritan thinking?*

The Puritans who settled in New England had a powerful apocalyptic system with two main axes: sacralized time and sacralized space. There could be many additional elements named here, but these two axes seem to me most important to comprehend the Puritan apocalyptic system. These axes are substantial and inseparable. By sacralizing time and space in their own specific apocalyptic and eschatological manner, Puritans were able to give meaning to and purpose for their migration to New England.

Sacralized Time

The idea of a sacralized time was not revolutionary. The 17th century Puritans did not invent or ad-lib a new paradigm or mode of thought, but they did put a special twist on it. They had a very unique take on sacralizing time and ecclesiastical history. They developed an ideology of history which explained their migration to and experience in the "wilderness" of colonial America. Three issues must be addressed when talking about sacralized time.

Firstly, the Puritan ideology of history was strongly influenced by Protestant historiography of the 16th century reformation. The reformation changed the perception of history and the understanding of the role of history dramatically. 16th century reformation not only reformed theology but also transformed the concept of history which the Puritans adopted. One of the major problems early Protestants encountered was that tradition and history seemed to speak for the cause of Catholicism. Indeed, Catholicism had dominated the 'western' world for roughly 1000 years. If the Catholics had supposedly misunderstood entire theological concepts that were then (re)discovered by Luther, where had the supposedly 'true' church been hiding for the scope of those years? This question was raised and many Protestants were at great pains to answer it by renegotiating the concept of history and finally coming to a new understanding of its role. In his work on Puritan history and apocalypse, Zakai notes:

Indeed, it was [the Protestants'] attempt to provide a historical basis for the break with the church of Rome, and to demolish the historical foundation upon which the papacy built its claim to exclusive power, that led the Protestants to launch their appeal to the study of history that became a major dimension of the Reformation itself. (Zakai 13)

Protestants, therefore, began to take up a perspective on history that was strikingly different from that of the Catholics. Protestants began to justify their agenda by historically documenting the 'true' church and likewise falsifying the Catholic agenda by historically making evident that the Church of Rome had not been the 'true' church.

Luther himself wrote in 1535: "[t]hough I was not at first historically well informed, I attacked the papacy on the basis of Holy Scripture. Now I rejoice heartily to see that others have attacked it from another source, that is, from history" (Firth 13). History was therefore in full accord with the Bible for Luther. Prophecy and fulfillment that had since been thought inside biblical categories now began to spill out into history. Thus, on the basis of *sola scriptura*, in the Protestant mind, the concept developed that history and prophecy went hand in hand. "[Protestants] succeeded in erasing the boundaries between sacred and secular history and uniting both into one history evolving along a special dimension of time in which promise leads to fulfillment, and prophecy to its realization" (Zakai 13). This concept is one of the elements that is pivotal in understanding the Puritan apocalyptic system.

19

This leads to a second issue: ecclesiastical history was established as being at the heart of all history. Cotton Mather wrote in 1702 in his famous *Ecclesiastical History of New England*:

I write the wonders of the Christian religion, flying from the depravations of Europe, to the American Strand. [...] But of all History it must be confessed, that the palm is to be given unto Church History; wherein the dignity, the suavity, and the utility of the subject is transcendent. (Miller and Johnson 167f)

Church history was the most eloquent form of 'universal' history and in fact was its mother for Mather. The course of the true saints of the true God was at the heart of his interest. He wanted to trace the trajectory of the unfeigned Christians, the genuine church, because this was where God provided guidance and leadership in the most direct manner. Church history, conclusively, was the pinnacle, the zenith of history in general.

It is important at this juncture to deal with the ecclesiology of Puritan sentiment, as it naturally ties in with their concept of history. The Greek term εκκλησια (ecclesia) entails the 'gathering of the called out ones,' which is used roughly 115 times in the New Testament to refer to the church. The church members were the ones who had been called out of the world into the presence of God through Christ himself, spoken in terms of the Holy Spirit. This definition of ecclesia pertains to the self-perception of Puritans. They viewed themselves as the body of Christ, leaning thereby heavily on the Epistle to the Ephesians (4:15f.). They were not solely a group of people who had similar beliefs, but viewed themselves as the body of Christ – and therefore, as the center of history.

Puritans thus found themselves caught up in a gigantic process of cosmic dimensions. God was watching the world and had his eyes fixed on what was happening with the Puritans. The Reformation conception of history led to the understanding of ecclesiastical history as the center of world history itself. Because the Puritans viewed themselves as the body of Christ, their actions had an impact and influence on all of history, no matter how small and limited their actions might have appeared to them or others.

A third point is that the Puritan perception of history was highly teleological, apocalyptic, and eschatological. Due to Jesus' arrival, history had been divided into two parts. All of history before Jesus' birth was directed towards his first coming. The Old Testament had prophesied and proclaimed a messiah and all of God's people had been awaiting the savior. After Christ's birth, death, and ascension, all history was now geared toward his second coming as prophesied in the New Testament. In this progress towards the second coming, the church had a significant role to play. It was the diamond in the rough – or, in Puritan terms – it was the 'small remnant' or 'pregnant woman' that would one day be caught up in God's glory in Christ's second coming (Isaiah 11, Revelation 12, I. Thessalonians). It would open the door to a new era. History, therefore, had a τελος (telos), namely Christ's second coming that would at last set everything "right." History was therefore not only teleological, but equally inherently apocalyptic and eschatological in the Puritan mindset. The true church of Christ stood amid the center of history and pointed its menacing finger towards the end. Thus, Puritans lived, in a real sense, not in the present, but rather in the aftermath of the past (Christ's first coming) and more significantly in the face of the future (Christ's second coming).

In sum, the Puritans' historiography had deemed history sacred and the 'true' church, as opposed to the Roman church, the central agency of history, which in turn, was directed towards its own end. Therefore, Puritan history and time had become sacralized which forms the first of our two axes.

Sacralized Space

The second important axis to understand the Puritan apocalyptic system is the sacralized state of space. There are two features that are vital to grasp this category. First, England had become de-sacralized and was considered as an apostate state. A very brief historical overview of how Puritans came to believe this shall be mentioned here (Ahlstrom 89-94). Under Henry VIII (1509-1547) England proclaimed its independence from the Church of Rome with the "Act of Supremacy" in 1534, which officially set off the Reformation of England. Edwards VI's (1547-1553) rather short reign, however, was the real watershed of the English Reformation, as he began to reinforce Protestantism. It is in this period that Puritanism was born. Once the Catholic Queen Mary I (1553-1558) succeeded Edward, all his efforts were soon shattered during the long and brutal six years of Mary's reign. The undertaking to 'puritanize' England was destroyed and Puritan hostility towards Queen Mary came quite natural. Queen Elizabeth (1558-1603), who was Protestant, succeeded her half-sister Mary and made a great effort to establish peace. Although Puritanism was able to flourish once again more freely, many were not pleased with her reign because she was not vigorous enough in pushing the Protestant Reformation any further, being perceived by many as rather 'luke-warm.' After her long reign, James I (1603-1625) succeeded and openly showed his disrespect for the Puritan cause. Finally in 1625 Charles I ascended to the throne of England and overtly attacked the Puritans. He married a Catholic and politically fought against the Puritans.

Eventually, by 1630, after a long back and forth, the Puritans began to grasp that England might no longer be the 'elect nation.' Seen from the perspective of sacralized time, England no longer was part of the ecclesiastical history. England had become de-sacralized. John Winthrop, the famous governor of Massachusetts, came to precisely this conclusion in the years after Charles I ascended to the throne. He wrote in 1629:

21

"if the Lord seeth it will be good for us, he will provide a shelter and a hiding place for us and ours as a Zoar for Lott, Sarephtah for his prophet" (Zakai 133). In this dense sentence, two different biblical images and narratives are interwoven. On the one hand Winthrop uses the story of Genesis 19, where Lot had to flee to Zoar from the city of Gomorrah in order to not be killed with the destruction of the evil city by God. On the other hand, he uses the story of the prophet Elijah (1. Kings 18), whom God sent to Zarephath, in order to save him from the rage of Ahab. Both of these references, however, show how Winthrop interpreted the migration from England to America: as an exodus from an evil and bad place. "In Winthrop's mind, therefore, the sacralization of America went hand in hand with the desacralization of England within the confines of the sacred history of the church" (Zakai 134). England, accordingly, had been offered the chance to establish the New Jerusalem, to bring about a sacred history in a sacred space. However, due to corrupt rulers, England had failed to live up to its calling. Thus, God had prepared a hiding place for ecclesiastical history to play out His design. The exodus from England was the only corollary.

This perspective, by way of contrast, differed decisively from the English Protestants in Virginia. Protestants in Virginia did not view their migration as an exodus, but rather as a genesis (Zakai 94-119). For them, England had not become de-sacralized, but remained sacred as God would work through Virginia to eventually proclaim the gospel to the entire world. It is interesting and important, hence, to emphasize that the Puritan view of their migration to the New World was not the only one when looking at the beginning of American history. The understanding that America was the last resort for a small remnant of pure Christians to flee to from a lost and apostate nation was appropriately and very uniquely Puritan.

The second feature with regard to the sacralization of space by the Puritans who set out for America is that their exodus not only entailed the idea of *escape* but also of *renewal*. In the axis of space, it was vital for the Puritans to portray their migration as a new beginning. Perry Miller noted:

These Puritans did not flee to America; they went in order to work out that complete reformation which was not yet accomplished in England and Europe, but which would quickly be accomplished if only the saints back there had a working model to guide them. (Miller 11)

One primary source that is of great importance in this context is the "General Observations for the Plantation of New England." It was a pamphlet written by a group of Puritans who explained the sacred meaning of their future migration to New England within the context of providential history. The authors wrote in the same year as Winthrop, that is in 1629:

2. All other Churches of Europe are brought to desolation, and our sins, for which the Lord begins already to frown upon us and to cut us short, do threaten evil times to be coming upon

us, and who knows, but that God hath provided this place to be a refuge for many whom he means to save out of the general calamity, and seeing the Church hath no place left to fly into but the wilderness, what better work can there be, than to go and provide tabernacles and food for her when she be restored. (Winthrop Society)

The end of the European churches is not rendered as destructive, but rather as the beginning of something new. The picture of the church fleeing into the wilderness is not a message of the end but of renewal. It rests on the biblical account of Revelation 12:1-6 in which a pregnant woman flees from the dragon (devil) to give birth to a child in the wilderness, the place that God had prepared for her. The Puritans drew upon this image to express their interpretation of their migration. They perceived themselves as fulfilling this prophecy, as the ones who were the pregnant woman, ready to give birth to a child that would eventually redeem the world. Their "errand into the wilderness" was not a sign of weakness but rather fulfilled a prophecy that promised renewal, birth, and life. The exodus from England was not a flight into the dark, but an errand into the sacred wilderness to prepare for the end and thereby the restoration of the world. Thus, the sacred space was a space of resurgence and renewal. In sum, the second axis (space) is held together on the one side by de-sacralizing England and on the other by impregnating the New World with hope of revival.

Conclusion

The Puritan perception of history is pivotal in understanding their migration to America. It was heavily influenced by the Protestant transformation of the concept of history and historiography of the 16th century and eventually gave birth to their notion of sacred ecclesiastical time. Secondly, the Puritan understanding of sacred space led them to discard England and de-sacralize it. Thus, America was sacralized as the wilderness that had been prophesied in the New Testament. It is in this context that certain phrases might ring a common tune: "errand in the wilderness," "We shall be a city upon a hill," "The eyes of all people are upon us," or even "God Bless America" and "In God We Trust." In all of these phrases, the ideas of sacred time and sacred space reverberate. Essentially, every Puritan thought can be located within these two axes.

Puritans were therefore the first to develop a purely American ideology that claimed self-reliance and autonomy. Being baptized in sacred time and sacred space, colonial America became a political and cultural entity of its own. In a word: Puritans were able to create a religious and ideological gulf between the Old World and their New World by focusing on the end of it.

Works Cited

Ahlstrom, Sydney E. *A Religious History of the American People*. New Haven and London: Yale UP, 1972. Print.

"General Observations for the Plantation of New England" (ca. 1628). *The Winthrop Society*. Web. 6 Sept. 2007.

Firth, Katharine R. *The Apocalyptic Tradition in Reformation Britain: 1530-1645*. Oxford: Oxford UP, 1979. Print.

Mather, Cotton. "Magnalia Christi Americana, A General Introduction." *The Puritans: A Sourcebook of Their Writings*. Eds. Perry Miller and Thomas H. Johnson. Vol. 1. New York: Harper, 1963. Print.

Miller, Perry. *Errand into the Wilderness*. Cambridge, Mass.: Belknap Press, 1956. Print.

Möhring, Hannes. *Der Weltkaiser der Endzeit*. Stuttgart: Jan Thorbecke Verlag, 2000. Print.

Zakai, Avihu. *Exile and Kingdom: History and Apocalypse in the Puritan Migration to America*. Cambridge: Cambridge UP, 1992. Print.

The World Caught Between *Good* and *Evil*: Elements of Evangelicalism in U.S. Foreign Policy

Raphaela Holinski

Since the evangelical revival of the 1970s, evangelicalism has become the most influential religious trend in the United States. According to a Gallup Poll in 2006, one hundred million Americans regarded themselves as evangelicals (Boyer, "Evangelical Dogmas"). In recent years they have become a force to reckon with in politics. Politicians have managed to accommodate them, incorporating some of their views in important issues and making use of a rhetoric geared towards the mindset of the Christian right.

My aim here is to examine how the evangelical body of thought and in particular the element of prophecy belief can be found in President George W. Bush's speeches on foreign policy. But before turning to these, a brief overview of evangelicalism, and, more specifically, the premillennial strand will be useful. According to the historian Paul Boyer, evangelicals are

Protestants who read the Bible literally as God's inerrant word; believe in the Second Coming of Christ; insist on a personal, or 'born again' religious experience; encourage missionary efforts; and apply a Manichean, black-and-white moral code to personal behavior, public affairs, and world events. (Boyer, "Evangelical Dogmas")

They are concerned with keeping God's laws in this life in order to belong to the chosen few in the next. In a world where all is relative, where growing secularization has eroded faith and traditional values, the evangelicals stand firm in their belief in an all-powerful God, in definitive categories of right and wrong and in life after death. This has consequences for their understanding of politics.

A central feature of evangelicalism is its prophetic belief system which is based on the idea that all human history unfolds according to God's plan; a plan which he has revealed in certain biblical texts. It is up to his true believers to decipher the texts and to identify the events of past, present and future. Up to the late eighteenth century the postmillennialist interpretation of the biblical prophetic texts dominated, as "specially favored of God, the New World would play a central role in bringing on the Millennium. Christ's return would crown a long period of growing Christian influence and diminishing tyranny – a process in which America would figure prominently" (Boyer, *When Time Shall Be No More* 75). This is the old idea of America's exceptionalism – a part of its 'manifest destiny.'

The current most popular version of prophecy belief among evangelicals is premillennial dispensationalism, which was developed by John Darby in the Nineteenth Century and holds sway in evangelical circles up to this day (Boyer, "John Darby Meets Saddam Hussein" B10). Darby taught that salvation history consists of a sequence of dispensations. These are epochs when God has entered into a covenant with the human race. Covenant after covenant has been broken due to the sinful nature of humankind and each time God has initiated a new dispensation. The current one will end with Christ's Second Coming and will be preceded by a series of catastrophic events. Christ will separate the believers from the non-believers. While the former will join Him in the Rapture, the latter will suffer under the seven year rule of the Antichrist. He will be defeated at the battle of Armageddon when Christ, ruling from a New Jerusalem, will set up a peaceful 1000 year reign on earth (Boyer, *When Time Shall Be No More* 80-112). This version of prophecy belief challenged the idea of American exceptionalism:

As Darby's premillennial dispensationalism became an increasingly important strand of U.S. prophecy writing, belief in America's special millennial destiny diminished accordingly … A few dissented or tried to soften the verdict, yet most post-1945 prophecy popularizers foresaw America's imminent destruction or drastic decline as recompense for its wickedness and unbelief. (Boyer, *When Time Shall Be No More* 244)

Thus, after 1945, prophecy writing concerned itself with the nation's perceived departure from the right path and consequent loss of the claim to its 'manifest destiny,' which was then transferred to the true believers. It was their mission to harvest as many souls as possible to create a global community of believers.

Premillennialism draws on biblical prophetic texts such as Daniel, Ezekiel, the 'Little Apocalypse' of Mark 13 and The Revelation of John. It is believed that, rightly understood, these texts can be used to tell us where we are in God's plan. Applied to world events, salvation history goes hand in hand with salvation geography which changes according to whom and where those currently identified as Christ's enemies are located. For example, salvation geography has taken on the biblical idea (from *Daniel,Revelation* and*Ezekiel*) of a northern kingdom, Gog, that will help the Antichrist in his rebellion against God. The possible identity of this kingdom has lent itself to various interpretations. During the Cold War Russia was held to be Gog (Boyer, *When Time Shall Be No More* 152ff.). More recently, since Saddam Hussein's invasion of Kuwait in 1990, the focus has been on the Middle East and Islam, and there has been a resurgence of the ancient belief that the Muslims, as descendants of Ishmael, represent *evil*, while the Jews, as descendants of Isaac, (and their supporters) represent *good* (Boyer, "Evangelical Dogmas"). Furthermore the importance of the foundation of Israel in 1948 has been emphasized, as premillennialists regard the Jewish settlements and the Israeli plan to rebuild the Temple in Jerusalem as part of God's great plan (Boyer, "John Darby Meets Saddam Hussein" B10).

As mentioned above, premillennialists do not reject a global spiritual community, but they distrust any secular global organizations and this has implications for their attitudes toward U.S. foreign policy. Indeed, such organizations as the United Nations or the International Monetary Fund are sometimes seen as the coming armies of the Antichrist and, although instrumental in the fulfillment of God's plan, are considered to be evil. Indeed, "many [prophecy writers] pinpointed the United Nations as the fore-runner of the prophesied world state. If not a protoworld government itself, Walvoord argued in 1964, the UN was playing a key prophetic role by eroding national loyalty and indoctrinating the masses in globalism" (Boyer, *When Time Shall Be No More* 264; for the paragraph cf. ibid. 207, 264, 295, 325).

There is a contradiction here: why distrust, or even act against the "evil" organizations, if they are to bring about God's will? Aware of this problem and not wishing to be accused of interference in God's plan, premillennialists initially kept out of politics and concentrated on family and community. However, in the 1970s there was a gradual shift towards involvement in local, national and international affairs. This was not immediately approved of by all the believers. But it was accepted by many and "[p]remillennialists who campaigned for nuclear disarmament or environmental protection justified *their position* on the grounds that such issues were important *in the present age*, even though human society and the earth itself would ultimately fall under God's judgment" (Boyer, *When Time Shall Be No More* 301). By 1980 the power of the politically organized Christian right under Jerry Falwell (the movement known as the 'Moral Majority') played a significant role in getting Ronald Reagan elected. Pat Robertson's Christian Coalition had and continues to have considerable influence through voters and substantial financial backing. In 2000, eighty percent of the religious conservatives voted for George W. Bush. This political engagement of a great number of such voters is something that U.S. politicians have had to take into account ever since. Just as they have to consider other lobbies important for their election campaigns they must now consider the Christian right when discussing political issues and making decisions (for this paragraph cf. Boyer, "God's Country?" 60f.)

In President George W. Bush's speeches there is considerable evidence of the influence of this evangelical body of thinking. I begin by quoting from his "Address to a Joint Session of Congress and the American People" on 20 September 2001, where, shortly after the attacks on the World Trade Center, Bush stated: "Every nation, in every region, now has a decision to make. Either you are with us, or you are with the terrorists." When he welcomed the French President to the White House on 6 November 2001, he elaborated on this statement: "[O]ver time, it's going to be important for nations to know they will be held accountable for inactivity. You are either with us or you are against us in the fight against terror." Even though the phrasing is a little different, this is a clear allusion to Jesus' words in the Gospel according to Mark 9:40: *For he that is not against us is on our part*, and in Luke 9:50: *For he that is not against us is for us*. The legitimate condemnation of the attack and the aim to unite all nations in a common endeavor to defeat terrorism is expressed in the dualistic rhetoric of the evangelicals. This results in a simplistic approach to the complicated area of terrorism. The problems are raised to a religious level where nothing can be rationally challenged. The biblical associations reinforce the idea that Bush knows and is carrying out God's will. The necessity for an in-depth analysis of the situation is rejected.

In his 20 September 2001 speech, the President explained to the Americans what the terrorists hate about the United States:

Americans are asking, why do they hate us? They hate what they see right here in this chamber – a democratically elected government. [...] They hate our freedoms [...] what is at stake is not just America's freedom. This is the world's fight. This is civilizations' fight. This is the fight of all who believe in progress and pluralism, tolerance and freedom. [...] Great harm has been done to us. We have suffered great loss. And in our grief and anger we have found our mission and our moment. ("Address to a Joint Session of Congress and the American People", 20 September 2001)

As a democratic, free country the U.S. must be 'good' and countries that do not have a similar democratic system must be enemies of freedom and thus evil. The U.S. mission is accordingly to defeat them and to convert them to democracy. America's 'manifest destiny' is made clear. This nationalistic argumentation is unlikely to win international support but will suit the evangelically-minded. It is, however, important to note that here "our mission and our moment," a.k.a. 'manifest destiny,' is used in the old, more inclusive sense of the entire nation's God-given role, which is where Bush departs from the premillennial prophecy belief outlined earlier. But since the premillennialists do believe in their missionary responsibility, they are likely to accept what Bush says here, albeit with some reservation.

In speech after speech Bush applies a Manichean moral code using biblical allusions and demonizing those states currently perceived as America's greatest enemies. For adherents of prophecy belief, states such as communist North Korea, dictatorial Iraq and theocratic Iran, which according to Bush "constitute an axis of evil, arming to threaten the peace of the world," become the army of the Antichrist as foretold in their salvation history. The President assures them that the U.S. "can overcome evil with greater good" ("State of the Union Address", 29 January 2002). Thereby he indicates (for evangelicals in the know) that America will take Paul's advice in his letter to the Romans (12:21): *Be not overcome of evil, but overcome evil with good*. The divine mission will be fulfilled: "Once again, we are called to defend the safety of our people, and the hopes of all mankind. And we accept this responsibility" ("State of the Union Address", 28 January 2003).

An example of the influence of premillennialist salvation geography is the following quotation taken from a speech President George W. Bush held in December 2005, in which he discussed the Iraqi election:

These acts are part of a grand strategy by the terrorists. Their stated objective is to drive the United States and coalition forces out of the Middle East so they can gain control of Iraq and use that country as a base from which to launch attacks against America, overthrow moderate governments in the Middle East, and establish a totalitarian Islamic empire that stretches from Spain to Indonesia. ("President Discusses Iraqi Elections, Victory in the War on Terror," 14 December 2005)

Surely this echoes an implicit reference of the premillennialists' idea of the Middle East as the northern kingdom that will help prepare the Antichrist's seven year rule on earth by extending its rule across the globe. Such words are meant to mobilize support for a war against God's enemies.

When it comes to the decision to disregard the U.N. Bush knows he can rely on the approval of the Christian Right. In a National Press Conference on 6 March 2003, the President proclaimed: "I'm confident the American people understand that when it comes to our security, if we need to act, we will act, and we really don't need United Nations approval to do so. [. . .] [W]hen it comes to our security, we really don't need anybody's permission." This argument is in accordance with the premillennialists' distrust of secular global organizations. What need of the approbation of others has a people with a claim to the possession of absolute truth and a divine mission?

As already mentioned, the Jews and the state of Israel have a special role in the premillennialists' version of the divine plan. It therefore comes as no surprise that the American President can be sure of approval when he appears as a staunch supporter of Israel. In a Prime Time News Conference on 11 October 2001 Bush makes the U.S. position clear:

I have met with Prime Minister Sharon, and I've assured him every time we've met that he has no better friend than the United States of America. [. . .] I believe there ought to be a Palestinian state, the boundaries of which will be negotiated by the parties, so long as the Palestinian state recognizes the right of Israel to exist and will treat Israel with respect, and will be peaceful on her borders. [. . .] We're working hard on the topic, [. . .]. It's a very important part of our foreign policy.

Adherents of pre-millennial prophecy belief may have no quarrel with this. But many others, even if endorsing his opinions, would welcome a more measured and analytic approach to the intractable problems involved.

I set out to show that elements of the evangelical body of thought as described by Paul Boyer can be found in President Bush's speeches on foreign policy. In his rhetoric he adopts the Manichean moral code and uses a religious frame of reference which lends itself to the premillennialists' self-perception as those who carry out God's will and are part of His divine plan. This leads them to accept the fight against *evil* and even to prefer military intervention to (in their eyes) fruitless negotiations with demonized adversaries. Although Bush's understanding of America's mission (the old idea of 'manifest destiny') is not identical to theirs, they can identify sufficiently with what he says to go along with his policies.

Attempts to establish and scrutinize the factors influencing the politics of a nation involve an analysis of its mindset. In the case of the U.S. we cannot neglect the religious perspective which has played an increasing role in recent decades. This is something Europeans, with their generally more secular outlook, are perhaps inclined to do.

Works Cited

Boyer, Paul. "Evangelical Dogmas, Innovative Strategies, Activist Politics: America's Post-1970 Religious Revival and Its Public-Policy Implications." German Association for American Studies. Ruhr-University Bochum, 31 May 2007. Print.

—. "God's Country? The Conservative Resurgence in Contemporary American Protestantism." *Europe and America*. Ed. Britta Waldschmidt-Nelson. Heidelberg: Universitätsverlag Winter, 2006. 51-68. Print.

—. "John Darby Meets Saddam Hussein: Foreign Policy and Bible Prophecy." *Chronicle of Higher Education* 49.23 (2003): B10-B11.

—. *When Time Shall Be No More: Prophecy Belief in Modern American Culture*. Cambridge, Mass.: Harvard UP, 1992. Print.

Buschschlüter, Siegfried. "I'm a War President." *Aus Politik und Zeitgeschichte* 14 (2006): 3-4. Print.

Bush, George W. "Address to a Joint Session of Congress and the American People." *The White House*. 20 Sept. 2001. Web. 20 May 2007.

—. Prime Time News Conference. *The White House*. 11 Oct. 2001. Web. 20 May 2007.

—. "America's Youth Respond to Afghan Children's Fund." *The White House*. 16 Oct. 2001. Web. 20 May 2007.

—. Welcoming of President Chirac to White House. *The White House*. 6 Nov. 2001. Web. 20 May 2007.

—. "State of the Union Address." *The White House*. 29 Jan. 2002. Web. 20 May 2007.

—. "State of the Union Address." *The White House*. 28 Jan. 2003. Web. 20 May 2007.

—. National Press Conference on Iraq. *The White House*. 6 Mar. 2003. Web. 20 May 2007.

—. "President Discusses Operation Iraqi Freedom at Camp Lejeune." *The White House*. 3 Apr. 2003. Web. 20 May 2007.

—. "President Discusses Iraqi Elections, Victory in the War on Terror." *The White House*. 14 Dec. 2005. Web. 29 May 2007.

—. "State of the Union Address." *The White House*. 23 Jan. 2007. Web. 29 May 2007.

Garrett, Crister S. "Ein Brückenschlag zwischen 'altem' und 'neuem' Europa." *Aus Politik und Zeitgeschichte* 14 (2006): 5-11. Print.

Goldhagen, Daniel J. *Hitler's Willing Executioners: Ordinary Germans and the Holocaust.* New York: Knopf, 1996. Print.

Hennes, Michael. "Der neue Militärisch-Industrielle Komplex in den USA." *Aus Politik und Zeitgeschichte* B46 (2003): 41-6. Print.

Homolar-Riechmann, Alexandra. "Pax Americana und gewaltsame Demokratisierung. Zu den politischen Vorstellungen neokonservativer Think Tanks." *Aus Politik und Zeitgeschichte* B46 (2003): 33-40. Print.

Minkenberg, Michael. "Die Christliche Rechte und die amerikanische Politik von der ersten bis zur zweiten Bush-Administration." *Aus Politik und Zeitgeschichte* B46 (2003): 23-32. Print.

Müller-Fahrenholz, Geiko. "Krieg nach Gottes Willen? Religiöse Wurzeln der gegenwärtigen amerikanischen Politik." *Deutsches Pfarrerblatt* 103 (2003): 283-8. Print.

Religion and Popular Music

Marilyn Manson – The All-American Antichrist? Prophecy Belief in U.S. Pop Culture

Moritz Schuster

And the world spreads its legs
For another fuckin' star!
'Cause I AM the all-american Antichrist.
I was made in america,
And america hates ME for what I am.

(Marilyn Manson, "Rock'n'Roll Nigger")

The intentions of Marilyn Manson are made clear in his 1995 adaptation of Patti Smith's song "Rock 'n' Roll Nigger" (1978). He wanted to become a star, an anti-hero, the "all-american Antichrist." And in the meantime, it can be argued that since that time, he has successfully done so.

Having entered the Billboard Top 50 with his debut album *Portrait of an American Family* in 1994 and the EP *Smells Like Children* in the following year, his sophomore album *Antichrist Superstar*, released in 1996, reached number three on the Billboard charts. His 1998 release *Mechanical Animals* and *The Golden Age of the Grotesque*, released in 2003, both achieved number one. His fourth album, *Holy Wood (in the Shadow of the Valley of Death)*, released in 2000, reached position 13. All releases mentioned here and a Marilyn Manson "best of" compilation as well as a live recording gained gold or platinum status in the U.S. ("Marilyn Manson Discography"). A vast number of mostly Evangelicals have been protesting against Marilyn Manson for more than ten years. Senator Joseph Liebermann of Connecticut underlined that "this is perhaps the sickest group ever promoted by a mainstream record company" (Jeffrey 3 in Manson 1998: 262 and Wright 375). And Marilyn Manson was among the first to be blamed after the massacre at Columbine High School in Littleton, Colorado (Burns).

Rock legends like Elvis Presley, the Rolling Stones and Alice Cooper, to name only a few, have shown that provocation can lead to success. Although Marilyn Manson also includes his variation of the 'sex, drugs and rock 'n' roll' concept and benefits from support by star-producer and label-owner Trent Reznor, his huge success in the U.S. is primarily rooted in the various ways in which he incorporates religious elements onto his band's construct. The band construct includes his whole performance, outfit, and imagery, but this paper will mainly focus on the religious allusions in his lyrics and rely for background information on his relationship to religion on the evidence that can be found in his autobiography *The Long Hard Road out of Hell*.

I will argue that Marilyn Manson has three major strategies of incorporating religious elements in the band construct that explain his success. First, he constructs his persona as the Antichrist, thus provoking Evangelicals and in particular premillennialists, effectively gaining the media's interest and publicity. Second, his frequent use of Christian elements not only provokes the Christian community in general, but at the same time makes it easy for most Americans to relate to his lyrics because it plays upon well known cultural imagery and myth. In addition to Christian mythology, he also alludes to bits and pieces from a wide range of old and new cultural myths, including Greek mythology, the Kabbalah, Tarot, or – from the realm of popular myths – the shooting of President Kennedy. Third, he offers his fans a substitute for or antidote to traditional religion, by presenting himself as the "God of Fuck" (Manson 1994: "Cake and Sodomy"), the Antichrist Superstar and, more generally, an antihero that is to be adored (Bostic), followed and believed in. Due to the limitations of this paper, only the first strategy will be analysed in greater detail here. I will show how Manson created an image or persona that was able to generate a huge amount of publicity. To do this I will – after a short glimpse on how prophecy belief influences American society – analyse how he constructed his persona as a superstar, as the Antichrist, and how he synthesized both into the Antichrist Superstar. Then I will show how press and public reacted to this self-representation, and prove that Manson created his persona intentionally to trigger these reactions. Finally, I will explain how and why Manson changed his image after *Antichrist Superstar*.

Prophecy Belief in the United States

According to Paul Boyer, "one cannot fully understand the American public's response to a wide range of international and domestic issues without bearing in mind that millions of men and women view world events and trends, at least in part, through the refracting lens of prophetic belief" (xii). In *When Time Shall Be No More* he presents impressive figures substantiating this point. In 2006 "62 percent of Americans," for example, "had 'no doubts' that Jesus will come to earth again" (2). Boyer shows that prophetic belief is spread in the U.S. through religious broadcasting, prophecy paperbacks, Christian bookstores, magazines, Evangelical seminaries and Bible schools, prophecy hotlines, Christian comic books, prophecy films, end-time kitsch like wrist watches or bumper stickers, Christian rock music, folk and gospel music, visual arts, and through secular mass culture like rock and pop music, movies and marketing campaigns (5-10). Also numerous internet sites are gaining in importance. Although prophecy belief is more likely to be found in the southern "Bible

Belt" (13) and "among the lower-income groups and those with less formal school-ing" (14), it can be considered a national phenomenon among all social groups (13 f.). Boyer describes "the world of prophecy belief as a series of concentric circles, at the center of which is a core group of devotees who spend much time thinking about the Bible's apocalyptic passages and trying to organize them into a coherent scenario" (2). Dwight Wilson "estimated the number of firmly committed *premillennialists* at 8 million" (ibid.). The second group (or "circle") is not so sure about the details but still believes that some insights to future events can be found in the Bible (ibid.). The third group, which forms the outer circle appears at first glance secular and not interested in prophecy, but is nevertheless more or less influenced and shaped by eschatological concepts (3).

Marilyn Manson's Antichrist Superstar

Bearing this in mind, it is not surprising that the concept behind Marilyn Manson's al-bum *Antichrist Superstar* hit a nerve and aroused much publicity. The album describes two parallel transformation processes. Marilyn Manson (i.e. his persona) evolves from "worm" into a superstar and at the same time from "worm" into the Antichrist. These two states of being are amalgamated at the end in the final state of the transformation: Antichrist Superstar. The CD is divided into three parts: "Cycle I – The Hierophant", "Cycle II – Inauguration of the Worm" and "Cycle III – Disintegrator Rising." It should be noted that by styling himself into the "I" of his lyrics, Marilyn Manson aims at the eradication of the difference between the "author" and the "speaker" of his texts. This allows discussion, indeed, about "Marilyn Manson's transformations," while it does not at all eradicate the difference between the performative persona Manson and the real-life Manson, as will be shown in the final part of this essay.

The role of the Greek Hierophant (or hierophantēs), the "chief priest of the Eleusinian mysteries," was to open the ceremony and "proclaim truce for the period of the mysteries" (*The Oxford Classical Dictionary*). In the context of the album, the Hierophant is the first cycle and its role is to prepare the listeners of the CD for the transformation of Marilyn Manson. The four songs of the first part deal with drugs, consumer society, hate, religion, suicide and the like. They are not about the transfor-mation yet, and the lyrics do not differ from the lyrics of Manson's first two releases. Thus their function is to remind the listener of the values and ideas Marilyn Manson represented before his transformation.

The transformation into the Antichrist starts with "Little Horn," the first song of the second cycle: "Out of the bottomless pit comes the little horn / Little horn is born." According to Revelation 17:8, a beast with seven heads and ten horns comes "out of the bottomless pit." This beast is called the red dragon in Revelation 12:3 and Satan and Devil in Revelation 12:9 (Kushner). "Little horn" is mentioned in Daniel 7:8 and

8:9. There it comes up among the horns of a beast with ten horns, three of which are rooted out for the little horn to take their place. So the little horn, which has "eyes like the eyes of man, and a mouth speaking great things" (Daniel 7:8), can be considered as being part of the Devil if the beast is identical to the beast mentioned in Revelation (Kushner).

In "Antichrist Superstar," the first song of the third cycle, Manson refers to the Greek hydra, a water serpent with a number of heads, which is very similar to the biblical beast. The text passage "Cut the head off / Grows back hard / I am the hydra / Now you'll see your star" suggests that the hydra in Manson's song has regenerative powers just like the beast in Revelation 13:3: "And I saw one of his heads as it were wounded to death; and his deadly wound was healed" (Kushner). By the end of this song, the transformation into the Antichrist is complete: "The time has come it is quite clear / Our antichrist / Is almost here... / It is done."

Manson frequently uses the image of the fallen angel by describing his wings, which best mark the process of his transformation into the Antichrist. In "Cryptorchid" his "back is changing shapes," in "Wormboy" "the world shudders as the worm gets its wings" and in "Antichrist Superstar" "the Angel has spread its wings." However, one has to note that the topic of shape and personality shifting is underlined by puzzling changes in Manson's use of perspective here. While he writes in all three songs – "Cryptorchid," "Wormboy," and "Antichrist Superstar" – about his transformation out of the first person perspective and addresses an unspecified "you," at the same time he writes about the worm in "Wormboy" and about the angel in "Antichrist Superstar" in the third person. Hence it is as if the persona is at the same time undergoing its own personality change, while watching this process from the outside and commenting on it to his more or less sympathetic observers (i.e. his listeners). Further complicating is the fact that the worm that becomes a fallen angel cannot be the same being as the Antichrist whom Manson describes like the biblical beast, at least if the Bible is followed literally, because they are two different beings: "And the great dragon was cast out, that old serpent, called the Devil, and Satan, which deceiveth the whole world: he was cast out into the earth, and his angels were cast out with him" (Rev 12:9). As a result, three different biblically inspired beings are interwoven in *Antichrist Superstar:* a fallen angel, the hydra (resembling Satan, the great beast, etc.) and the little horn, which possibly belongs to the hydra but is not identical with it. Switching the narrative perspective and the imagery, Manson does not explicitly point out which role he plays. Possibly he plays all three roles in a kind of "unholy trinity" that represents the Antichrist as a counterpart to the holy trinity of Father, Son and the Holy Spirit (Kushner for another suggestion of an unholy trinity in *Antichrist Superstar).* As a result, *Antichrist Superstar* appears as a text that is highly open for interpretation.

While cycles two and three show Manson's transformation from worm into Antichrist, the transformation from worm to superstar is depicted in cycle two and also starts with the song "Little Horn," where the "world spreads its legs for another star." In "Deformography" he is already "a dirty [...] rock star" and in "Mr. Superstar" this transformation is complete. There he is adored by his "number one fan,," who refers to him as "Mr. Superstar," "Mr. Porno Star," "Mr. Supergod" etc.

The song "1996" in the third cycle finally shows how Antichrist and superstar amalgamate into Antichrist Superstar: "Anti people now you've gone too far / Here's your Antichrist Superstar." The title refers to the year in which *Antichrist Superstar* was released and is supposed to be a signal for the listener that the 'rise' of the Antichrist Superstar is a real event that takes place with the release of the album.

Marilyn Manson's The Long Hard Road out of Hell

The same dual transformation amalgamating into Antichrist Superstar that was portrayed in the album is described in Manson's autobiography *The Long Hard Road out of Hell*, which was published two years later in 1998. The text is also split in three parts: "Part One: *When I Was a Worm*," "Part Two: *Deformography*" and "Part Three: *How I Got My Wings*."

Already in the first sentence he plays upon the later transformation into the Antichrist by saying "Hell to me was my grandfather's cellar" (3). He reports that he feared after prophecy seminars in his Christian school that he might be the Antichrist (18-19) and concludes "the seeds of who I am now had been planted" (22). He describes the beginning of his transformation as starting just before he began high school with a re-interpretation of a death: "That last night in Canton, I knew that Brian Warner was dying. I was being given a chance to be reborn" (32). This quote is an allusion to John 3:7: "I tell you the truth, no one can see the kingdom of God unless he is born again." But as he sees himself born again as the Antichrist, it turns the concept of born again Christians upside down. In the second part of his autobiography, he already identifies himself with the Antichrist. Thus he directly alludes to Revelation 13:17 – "so that no one could buy or sell unless he had the mark, which is the name of the beast or the number of his name" – when he describes his after-show behaviour:

Near the end of our shows I used to smear my face with red lipstick and, if there were girls near the front of the stage I wanted to meet, I'd grab them and make out with them, *leaving on their faces the mark of the beast*, which served as an *entrance ticket to the hell* that was and always will be backstage. (172, my emphasis)

Whereas the mark in Revelation is needed to buy or sell any kinds of goods, the mark mentioned in Manson's autobiography "buys" an entrance ticket to his backstage room. In the third part he describes the final stage of his transformation by recalling a series of dreams he had of himself as the Antichrist. He concludes "I believe in dreams. [...] I dreamt I was the Antichrist, and I believe it" (212 f.).

Parallel to his transformation from worm into the Antichrist, he describes his transformation from worm into superstar. In the first part he is a more or less normal young boy who eventually comes into contact with "black magic, heavy metal, self-mutilation and conspicuous drug consumption" (40). He unsuccessfully tries to become a writer, has to deal with average teenager problems, experiences drugs and gradually gathers the first line-up of Marilyn Manson and the Spooky Kids in the second part. In the third part he is already successful with his band and strives for superstar status with *Antichrist Superstar*. He concludes: "The album had entered the pop charts at number three, and now I was bigger than rock clubs, rock cocaine and feel-good rock. [...] To some people, I was even bigger than Satan" (244).

In his autobiography, *Antichrist Superstar* is not the final stage of his transformation, but a rock album that is about his transformations. Manson writes that "my plan then was to write an album about the transformation I had endured" (219) and concludes that "all these things became the album *Antichrist Superstar*" (215). He sees *Antichrist Superstar* "essentially as a pop album – albeit an intelligent, complex and dark one" (232). As both transformations ultimately culminate in the record, it can also be regarded as a synthesis of Antichrist and superstar.

The reactions toward his self-representation show that his concept of provocation was very effective and helped him to utilise the potential of the media. Protesters distributed a prayer before a Marilyn Manson concert in Orlando, Florida, which stated that "the 'rock' group Marilyn Manson consists of demons or evil Spirits in that they espouse heretical beliefs, claim to be Antichrists and Satanists, and attempt to tempt children away from Christianity with sin" (Manson 1998: 248). A coalition led by William Bennett, co-director of the conservative lobby group Empower America, democratic senator Joseph Liebermann and C. Dolores Tucker, chairwoman of the National Political Congress of Black Women, tried unsuccessfully to stop Interscope from distributing Manson's records (Wright 375). The American Family Association, the Christian Family Network and others launched campaigns against Marilyn Manson. They accused him of killing live animals and abusing children on stage and other criminal acts (Wright 375f. and Manson 1998: 246-266). Another incident that shows how much impact the self-stylisation of Marilyn Manson as the Antichrist had on some people occurred one week before a Marilyn Manson performance in Florida. The TV show *Real Stories of the Highway Patrol* showed the arrest of a "twenty-five-year-old Christian fanatic with missing teeth", who had "a trunk full of guns" and "said he was going to Florida to kill the Antichrist" (Manson 1998: 263).

Manson wanted to provoke just these reactions in order to arouse enough publicity to actually become a superstar. Yet he always knew what he was doing and he created his Antichrist persona deliberately in every detail: "Marilyn Manson was the perfect story protagonist for a frustrated character like myself" (79). He learned the 'prophetic vocabulary' from the seminaries he attended at his Evangelical school and when he formed the band in 1989, he

was reading books about philosophy, hypnosis, criminal psychology and mass psychology (along with a few occult and true crime paperbacks) [...] As a performer, I wanted to be the loudest, most persistent alarm clock I could be, because there didn't seem like any other way to snap society out of its Christianity- and media-induced coma. (Manson 1998: 80)

Later, he writes, he was reading books "on the apocalypse, numerology, the Antichrist, and the Kabbalah" (227). When he comes to Anton Szandor LaVey, who made him a reverend of the Church of Satan, he reveals how LaVey makes use of society's beliefs and fears to achieve fame. "All the power LaVey wielded he gained through fear – the public's fear of a word: *Satan*. By telling people he was a Satanist, LaVey became Satan in their eyes – which is not unlike my attitude toward becoming a rock star" (165). This approach to becoming a rock star can be understood in a well-known analogy to the creation myth of the Bible: "In the beginning was the Word, and the Word was with God, and the Word was God" (John 1:1).

At present, the sites of the campaigns launched against Marilyn Manson by the Christian Family Network and others cannot be found on the internet anymore. This is no surprise. Once Manson had gained the media's attention, he had to become acceptable to the mainstream market to reach the highest chart positions. One of the steps to achieve this goal was to give interviews that contradicted the image he had at that time. So he told *Religion Today* in November 1997 that he had "never been [and] never will be a Satan worshipper or someone who worships the Devil, adding that he still considers himself a member of St Paul's Episcopal Church in his hometown of Canton, Ohio" (in Wright 374 f.). Consequently, Manson's lawyers took legal action against those 'false accusations,' receiving support from various North American civil liberties organisations (ibid. 375 f.). That explains why those internet sites have disappeared.

Thirteen months after the interview with *Religion Today*, Manson released his autobiography, which again portrays him as Antichrist Superstar. Some months later, he released his next album *Mechanical Animals* which shows him as Jesus Christ.The video clips for *Holy Wood* and the "Tainted Love" cover single he released after that again stylize him as the Antichrist. This makes sense when following the theory that Manson not only has to serve his fan base, which is more or less opposed to the mainstream, and the press, which is hungry for sensation and provocation, but also the more conservative mainstream. As a result, he has to oscillate between those two poles, between provocation and denial. An announcement he made after performing his first radio single "Sweet Dreams" at Toronto's Warehouse in October 22, 1996 shows him acutely aware of the differences among his fans: "That one was for the Top 40 crowd" (ibid. 379).

41

Conclusion

This paper has shown that the huge leap in success from Marilyn Manson's first two releases to *Antichrist Superstar* was mainly due to his self-representation as the Antichrist. He constructed his persona in minute detail in his lyrics, his autobiography and every other possible representation to the public. As a result of this provocation, his popularity rose significantly which in the end massively contributed to his record sales. Once he gained the media's attention, he changed towards a less provocative image in order to be attractive to the mainstream market as well. His other two strategies mentioned in the introduction also contributed to his success and have played an important role up to now, while the Antichrist-stylization strategy described in this paper is no longer as relevant for his success as it used to be. He still incorporates apocalyptic elements, as the video clip for "Disposable Teens" has shown, but his persona and overall image change with every album. Now that Marilyn Manson is highly successful, it does not seem to be important anymore that his persona is linked to one specific outrageous meaning ("Antichrist"), but rather that he keeps presenting something provocative to which the public can relate. However, Marilyn Manson's references to Biblical imagery have remained an important basis for his lasting success. This can be seen, for instance, also from his record *Eat Me, Drink Me*, released on 1 June 2007, which entered the charts at position eight. The title immediately reminds one of the last supper in Luke 22 with Manson giving his body and blood. His business model obviously still seems to work.

Works Cited

Bostic, Jeff Q. et al. "From Alice Cooper to Marilyn Manson: The Significance of Adolescent Antiheroes." *Academic Psychiatry* 27.1 (2003): 54-62. Print.

Boyer, Paul. *When Time Shall Be No More: Prophecy Belief in Modern American Culture.* 1992. Cambridge, Mass.: Harvard UP, 2000. Print.

Burns, Gary. "Marilyn Manson and the Apt Pupils of Littleton." *Popular Music and Society* 3 (1999): 3-8. Print.

Hornblower, Simon, and Antony Spawforth, eds. *The Oxford Classical Dictionary.* 3rd ed. Oxford: Oxford UP, 1996. Print.

Jeffrey, D. "MCA, Seagram assailed for graphic lyrics." *Billboard* 108 (1996). Print.

Kushner, Nick et al. "The Third and Final Beast." *The Nachtkabarett.* 2004. Web. 11 Jun. 2007.

Manson, Marilyn. *Portrait of an American Family.* Compact Disc. Nothing, 1994.

—. *Smells Like Children.* Compact Disc. Nothing, 1995. CD.

—. *Antichrist Superstar.* Compact Disc. Nothing, 1996. CD.

Manson, Marilyn with Neil Strauss. *The Long Hard Road out of Hell.* London: Plexus, 1998. Print.

"Marilyn Manson Discography." *Wikipedia.* 1 Jun. 2011. Web. 7 Jun. 2007.

Wright, Robert. "'I'd Sell You Suicide': Pop Music and Moral Panic in the Age of Marilyn Manson." *Popular Music* 19.3 (2000): 365-85. Print.

The Style/Content Dissonance: The Use of Popular Culture in Evangelical Music Production

Cornelius Herz

In her study *Shaking the World for Jesus: Media and Conservative Evangelical Culture* (2004), Heather Hendershot focuses on evangelical media production and scrutinizes to what extent and in which ways evangelical cultural production engages with the secular market. In the realm of music, she examines bands that are part of both the secular and the evangelical markets, for example, Sixpence-None-the-Richer or Creed. Does this cross-over to the secular market also indicate the secularization of the beliefs of these bands? Even though secularization might seem a straightforward answer, this would be too simple. As Hendershot points out: "over the course of the past thirty years Christian media have become not more secular but more ambiguous and [...] incredibly uneven in the degree to which they overtly proclaim their faith" (7). This ambiguity may range anywhere between direct references to their faith (no ambiguity at all) and complete avoidance to sing about "Satan, sex, parental disobedience, and other Christian bogeymen" (highest level of ambiguity, Hendershot 62). In other words if they do not refer to overtly Christian topics, they nevertheless never overstep the boundaries of Christian decency. We can conclude that on a textual level all of these bands remain within the evangelical fold – even if only via ambiguity.

Interestingly though, problems may arise if the music of some Christian bands is taken into consideration. Hendershot points toward the contradiction arising from sole concentration on the words: "it is supposedly all about the lyrics. In theory, then, a Christian hard-core band like Oblation can sing a death metal song that is antiabortion, and even though their thrashing beat feels violent, their antideath lyrics will redeem the song. What listeners make of this style/content dissonance is an unresolved question" (71). Hence, while the content of the music can always be seen as evangelical, the origin of the style of the music (the genre) is not necessarily evangelical – a veritable "style/content dissonance," as Hendershot calls it in the quote above.

This paper will focus on this dissonance – on music with a content that can be classified as evangelical and a style that can be classified as secular. In this context I will argue, firstly, that this dissonance serves as a means of convergence/integration *and* divergence/disintegration. Secondly, I will show that beyond these functions there is a subversive potential in this dissonance. Thirdly, I will demonstrate that it is especially the interaction with secular music that opens a space beyond ambiguous lyrics and wholesome texts. In order to substantiate my theses, I will use the songs of the band Saviour Machine as an example.

My definition of "evangelicalism" is derived from the renowned German compendium of religion *Religion in Geschichte und Gegenwart (Religion Past and Present)*:

Evangelikale Theologie kann abgegrenzt werden durch ihre vierfache Verpflichtung auf das griechische ευαγγελιον (Evangelium): 1. die grundlegende Bedeutung der Erlösung durch den persönlichen Glauben an Christus als den Herrn; 2. die letztgültige Autorität der Schrift für den Glauben und das Leben; 3. eine Lebensführung der Frömmigkeit und der Nachfolge; 4. ein aktives Engagement für Evangelisation und Dienst am Nächsten. (Johnston)

According to this excerpt, the four pillars of evangelicalism are the redemption through the personal belief in Christ (1.), the unquestionable authority of Scripture (2.), piety as well as the imitation of Christ (3.), and evangelization and brotherly love (4.). In the case of the band Saviour Machine, the authority of God's word (2.) is particularly revealing. If it is considered to be ultimate, the impact of the content of the Bible on every-day life has to be accepted. Here it is especially the belief in the predictions of the scripture concerning the end of the world which is typical of evangelicals. In fact, Paul Boyer points out that "[a]mong U.S. Protestants, prophecy belief usually comes embedded within a larger religious matrix that goes by the label 'evangelicalism'" (3). This concept of the end of the world normally features "the story of the Rapture: saved people are suddenly removed from the earth; the Antichrist rises to power and torments newly converted Christians during seven years of 'Tribulation'; and, finally, after the Battle of Armageddon, the Second Coming of Christ occurs" (Hendershot 178). As we will see, the revelation is pivotal for analyzing Saviour Machine.

Saviour Machine: Freaky Preachers or Lost Sheep?

Saviour Machine offers an interesting evangelical paradigm for a band "off the beaten track." They can be categorized as "epic metal,", "opera-," "progressive-," or "gothic-rock" – all genres normally not associated with evangelical music. This becomes obvious when the lead singer, Eric Clayton, enumerates their early musical influences: "We came from a background listening to Pink F[loyd], Black Sabbath, King Crimson, Led Z[eppelin]" (Coles). Still, Saviour Machine also has evangelical roots as Clayton mentions:

I was raised in a Southern Baptist church, so I had a heavy legalistic upbringing, heavy fire and brimstone kind of stuff. But at the same time there was a lot of passion and a lot of love. [...] Even though I turned my back on God and was very rebellious, I never really lost my faith in God [–] I just turned my back on Him. I thank God that I never did lose my complete faith because in the end, faith is what brought me home; faith, utter confusion, and desperation. (Coles)

Right here, we can already see the basis for the style/content dissonance: While the band is rooted in an evangelical upbringing, the first musical influences are rather of a secular nature.

With this (musical-) biographical background in mind, we can now focus on the musical production of the band itself to investigate the style/content dissonance. If we look at the content first, it seems to be quite obvious that Saviour Machine sings about evangelical topics, for example, in "The Promise:" "Lord, set your sanctuary in our midst forevermore / See us as we are lost in the day / The truth come forth we pray, o Lord / Bring us our eternal destiny, redeem the earth / From the curse of sin and suffering; we sing 'Maranatha'" (Saviour Machine). "Maranatha" is the Aramaic call for the Second Coming of Christ and hence for the Last Judgment, which found its place in Christian liturgy:

The celebration of the Lord's Supper as anticipation of the heavenly meal with the Messiah-Son of man in the coming Kingdom of God, even to the point of preserving in the liturgy the Aramaic exclamation *maranatha* ('O Lord, Come') and its Greek parallel *erche kyrie* ('Come, Lord!') as the supplicant calling for the Parousia (Second Coming) – all this became tradition. (Christianity)

Even if this expression is rooted in Christian tradition in general, its connotations are especially important to evangelical beliefs. As already pointed out when defining evangelicalism (Johnston's pillar no. 2), Bible prophecy plays a crucial part, and the Second Coming is the essential and promised return of Christ in glory or, in other words, the final victory of all believers. "Maranatha," then, is the call to fulfill the promise of redemption.

The song ends with the words: "Occupy until I come ..." (Saviour Machine) and echoes the King James translation of Luke 19:13 where Jesus exhorts his followers by means of a parable to use their potential until he comes back in the Parousia. This brings us back to two other points of the definition of evangelicalism given above: In order to be saved, one needs to "occupy", i.e. to follow or imitate, Christ (Johnston's pillar no. 3). What this also shows, then, is that the individual belief in Christ (Johnston's pillar no. 1), who is the way through which mankind is redeemed, is the only way to salvation. Apparently, with such keywords, a clearly evangelical message is rendered.

The lyrics, thus, do not seem to be ambiguous at all. Yet, other bands from a similar musical background use comparable language – even if they are far from being evangelical. The name of the band HIM, which at a first glance could be taken as an allusion to Jesus (or God), for example, stands for "His Infernal Majesty," and they named one of their CDs "Your Sweet Six Six Six" – all of which clearly shows that they consider themselves not to be evangelical. Still, they are listed in the same reference books for the gothic scene as Saviour Machine, for instance in *Das Gothic- und Dark Wave-Lexikon*, and, interestingly, HIM's song titles show an obvious linguistic similarity to the ones of Saviour Machine. They read "The Sacrament," "Resurrection," or even "Face of God." This is indeed the same diction which Saviour Machine uses, even if it is quickly turned upside down by HIM's, who also called one of their songs "Our Diabolikal [sic] Rapture" (A-Z Lyrics Universe).

Yet, as Eric Clayton says, both Saviour Machine and bands like HIM remain within the same system: "It's a very fine line from one side and the other. Believe it or not, it's much easier for a true Satanist to become a Christian, than [for] an atheist to become a Christian. The reason being is because if you're a true Satanist, you have to believe in God" (Coles). Thus, both bands are using ambiguous lyrics and certain expressions which cannot be said to belong only to the one end of the spectrum or to the other. Even if Saviour Machine appears to be blatantly evangelical, it is not *just* their personal belief but *also* the textual conventions of their musical environment that demand religion-based lyrics in the broadest sense. The consequence is ambiguity – but only up to a certain degree, i.e. even if the border is close, it is never crossed: For Saviour Machine, the Rapture will always be "divine" and never "diabolical."

Shifting our attention from content to style, Saviour Machine's "musical neighborhood," Gothic rock, is a successor of regular rock music or rock-n-roll, both of which are normally not connected to evangelical culture. Therefore, by playing gothic rock, Saviour Machine musically interacts with the secular sphere. Still, musical divisions are not as clear-cut as it may seem. Again, there is an ambiguity – especially if we take a look at further elements or facets of the style of Saviour Machine instead of just considering the genre itself, namely use of symbols, outward appearance and performance. Style is not limited to mean the musical genre alone but includes other elements through which a band may communicate with the world around them.

Saviour Machine is – at least sometimes – on tour with many bands who do not belong to the evangelical spectrum. Eric Clayton says: "We're probably one of the only [sic] Christian bands that get the opportunity to play certain festivals. [...] There were like 40,000 people attending this show. Bands like Slayer, Deicide [!], Cannibal Corpse, Motor Head, just about every band you can think of was playing" (Coles). Saviour Machine, then, participates in the performances of bands and with musicians who have nothing to do with evangelicalism or who are even opposed to it. This becomes immediately obvious if one visits the websites of the other bands. Deicide, for instance – the name alone is telling – features an inverted cross (deicide.com), thus clearly announcing their inversion of Christian values. Nonetheless, with the use of the cross they display their derivation from and relation to Christian origins. In this way, they use the same symbolic repertoire as that of an evangelical band like Saviour Machine, only that they use it with a difference.

Of course, one could say that Deicide's cross is obviously inverted and thus not really ambiguous enough. But, when looking at the outward appearance, especially of Eric Clayton, co-founder and lead singer of Saviour Machine, similarities between the evangelical band and non-evangelical ones are striking. Clayton is often depicted wearing a long black frock, his bald head covered with white make-up. Additionally, he may wear jewelry, e.g. earrings in the form of a cross (Clayton). With such a complexion and outfit, he is certainly not alone in the gothic scene. A check of Matzke's and Seeliger's reference book for the gothic subculture shows many artists dressed and made up in a similar way, for example the non-evangelical band Scarecrow ("Scarecrow").

From outward appearance, it is only a small step to performative qualities, where looks are important as well. Performance is a point, Eric Clayton recalls, where non-evangelical bands doubted Saviour Machine would reach the needed level of ambiguity, but where Saviour Machine proved them wrong:

We've had different reactions with different bands. Most of the time, after you get further into the tour and you get talking, they'll say: 'Before we did this tour we thought that you were going to be these freaky Christians, preaching around to everybody, and we felt really weird to be around you guys, but you guys are really cool. We didn't know what to expect from you musically or visually,' and that sort of thing. (Coles)

As we have seen, the style/content dissonance in relation to Saviour Machine not only includes the discordance between their pious lyrics and their secular music. Even if this contradiction is basic, it is important to stress that on both, the stylistic (in all its meanings) and the textual levels, ambiguity is a factor that multiplies Saviour Machine's possibilities to interact with the secular and the evangelical sphere in a never-ending game of approaching and stretching the thin red line between the religious and the worldly without ever crossing it completely.

Four Functions of the Style/Content Divide

The results of these oscillations in the productions of Saviour Machine are the paradoxical functions of the style/content dissonance: On the one hand this dissonance serves as a means of convergence and integration with both the inside and the outside of the evangelical culture: It functions to tie the band and its listeners to the evangelical world. This link is established especially by the lyrics. As long as 'sex, drugs, and rock-n-roll' are not mentioned, the band remains within the fold. But the style/content dissonance also functions to tie the band and its listeners to the secular sphere. This link is provided by the music itself, because it comes from this sphere.

On the other hand it also serves as a means of divergence and disintegration: The content (that does not match the style) allows a divergence from the profane world in that the lyrics never cross the line of referencing anything of an anti-evangelical nature. Yet the style, which diverges from the rather tame content, also allows a divergence from the pious sphere in that the style may be considered to be infested by unholy values – just consider the fact that in evangelical circles the question was seriously debated whether rock-n-roll music was inherently satanic (Hendershot 55).

These functions reflect Hendershot's description of evangelicals as "in but not of the world" (212). The style/content dissonance would allow them to exactly negotiate this weird and somewhat indefinable space of "in but not of." With regard to this characterization, the non-evangelical music should be considered far more a part of, rather than resisting evangelical life styles (a point which can also be made for other media, as Hendershot has shown in her book). Evangelicals make concessions to an overwhelming secular influence, but they remain true to their roots as well and try to incorporate both identities and attempt to make secular ways suitable for evangelical life. Eventually, this might help to lessen the bands' alienation from the general culture of the United States, allowing them to identify with it – or even to sanctify it. *Ambiguity* is the way that leads to these goals and that helps to avoid clear-cut divisions – thus, the functioning of the style/content dissonance may fulfill the seemingly contradictory purposes of cultural convergence and divergence at the same time.

The Further Potential of the Style/Content Dissonance

Yet, I would also argue that beyond these functions there is a greater potential in the style/content dissonance. The example of Saviour Machine shows that their musical style is neither a part of the general US-American mainstream nor of the evangelical one. This means that there is a subversive potential implied in the general style that may be transposed into the realm of evangelical music and culture. The general subversiveness of the musical style with all the different categories it comprises may challenge, contradict, or even defy the hegemonic mainstream of U.S. musical culture in general – and within the evangelical world, it will also offend the hegemonic norms and standards of the evangelical mainstream.

In a way then, Saviour Machine's music also carries a message that may serve not only as a way of connecting and disconnecting the band and their listeners to/from the secular and evangelical mainstream – but also as a way of relating their music to a specific part of a culture that may be detached from or even opposed to the secular *and* evangelical mainstream as a sort of subsystem of culture or even as a counterculture.

This function hints at the fact that evangelicals, just as the highly diverse general U.S. culture, also do not constitute a homogeneous group. This also means that gothic-induced convergence and integration as well as diversion and disintegration do not only occur in the mainstream but also in subgroups such as the evangelicals.

Towards a New Level of Ambiguity

Finally, it is especially the interaction with secular music genres and performances that opens a space beyond ambiguous, but tame lyrics and wholesome evangelical texts. In their music and performance style, evangelical bands can easily go much further than the highest levels of textual ambiguity – not to mention "evangelical bogeymen" (Hendershot 62). Here they may not only *leave* the grounds of evangelical culture but can go even further and *leave the general mainstream*. The choice of instruments in a band may instantly connect the music to a specific non-evangelical (sub)group and its specific music; already the first ten seconds of a song can decide which tradition a band would like to see itself. Evangelicals may not sing like worldly bands *about* sex, drugs, and rock-n-roll as desirable goals in life – even if using the highest level of ambiguity. But, they may produce *the same music, dress* in a similar way, and convince with a *comparable performance* that they are connected to the scene in which sex, drugs, and rock-n-roll play a decisive role.

And the result is more than imitation. Since evangelical bands such as Saviour Machine productively process their reality in two spheres (instead of merely remaining in and copying one), the textual ambiguities combined with the greater possibilities of the stylistic musical and performance ambiguity enable them to create and relate their own identity beyond the religious and the secular, existing somewhere in-between.

Works Cited

Boyer, Paul. *When Time Shall Be No More: Prophecy Belief in Modern American Culture.* Cambridge, Mass.: Harvard UP, 1992. Print.

"Christianity. The Church and Its History. Church Tradition." *Encyclopaedia Britannica.* Deluxe Edition 2004. London: Encyclopaedia Britannica: 2004. CD-ROM.

Coles, Mike. "Interview with Eric Clayton of Saviour Machine." 28 Dec. 1998. Web. 3 Jun. 2007.

Hendershot, Heather. *Shaking the World for Jesus: Media and Conservative Evangelical Culture.* Chicago: U of Chicago P, 2004. Print.

"HIM." *Das Gothic- und Dark Wave-Lexikon. Die schwarze Szene von A-Z.* Ed. Peter Matzke and Tobias Seeliger. Rev. ed. Berlin: Schwarzkopf & Schwarzkopf, 2003. Print.

Johnston, Robert K. "Evangelikale Theologie." *Religion in Geschichte und Gegenwart: Handwörterbuch für Theologie und Religionswissenschaft.* Ed. Hans Dieter Betz, Don S. Browning, Bernd Janowski, and Eberhard Jüngel. 4th, rev. ed. 9 vols. Tübingen: Mohr, 1998. Print.

"Saviour Machine." *Das Gothic- und Dark Wave-Lexikon. Die schwarze Szene von A-Z*. Ed. Peter Matzke and Tobias Seeliger. Rev. ed. Berlin: Schwarzkopf & Schwarzkopf, 2003. Print.

Saviour Machine. "The Promise." *DarkLyrics*. 2001. Web. 10 Jul. 2007.

"Scarecrow." *Das Gothic- und Dark Wave-Lexikon. Die schwarze Szene von A-Z*. Ed. Peter Matzke and Tobias Seeliger. Rev. ed. Berlin: Schwarzkopf & Schwarzkopf, 2003. Print.

Religion and Television

Reaching out to the Masses: An Analysis of the Evangelical Television Series *Family First*

GUNNAR BERNDT

Ever since the 1980s, Christian media in the United States has been continuously on the rise. Fundamentalists have successfully used print, radio, video, television, internet and other means of communication to spread their views and reinforce them (Hendershot, 2000: 152-154). A vast amount of such media specifically addresses the youth since, as Hendershot points out, "parents recognize that during the rebellious teen years their children may drift from their faith. Adults consider teens the most fragile links in the fundamentalist chain, and this is why so much media is directed to them" (2002: 101f.).

One interesting example is the sitcom/drama series *Family First*, which was a regular feature of the monthly television program *Fire by Nite,* aired on the evangelical Trinity Broadcasting Network in the 1990s. *Family First* primarily revolves around the show's main protagonist Doug Collins, an evangelical teen played by renowned youth minister Blaine Bartel, and his family, friends and acquaintances. In this paper, I will be discussing one single episode that illustrates in exemplary fashion, the specific qualities of this series. In the episode in question, Doug's friend Jonathan has just been tested positive for HIV, which, as it turns out, was transmitted to him by a girl named Susan, who in turn had been infected by Ty, the boy she had previously dated. Ty, who identifies as bisexual, has deliberately been spreading the virus and is currently seeing Cheryl, with whom Doug recently broke up because she suggested pre-marital sex. Doug hears about Ty's bisexuality from his friend Clarence, who is appalled after having become the object of one of Ty's sexual advances. In a second plot line, Amy, a close friend of Doug's sister Connie, has been impregnated and feels pressured into having an abortion before eventually deciding to keep the baby.

In conducting a "close viewing" of the episode whose plot I have just summarized, I will establish the function of *Family First* as a Christian fundamentalist tool directed at young viewers. More specifically, I will outline the show's advocacy of opposition to three central sins as identified by Christian fundamentalism – namely pre-marital sex, homosexuality (Don S. Browning et al., 236) and abortion (Craig A. Rimmerman, 122). In addition to stating the obvious, however, I also intend to undertake a characterization of the approach taken by the show in addressing these issues. While fundamentalists have a reputation of drawing their moral values from what

55

they regard as the literal readings of selective Bible passages, I am going to argue that the approach taken by *Family First* is of an entirely different nature. Rather than attempting an outright Bible-based condemnation of sin, the show predominantly hides its religious aims under a secular plot and thereby sends only ambiguously religious messages while making use of images and music intended to influence viewers. Indeed, one might go so far as to contend that the *sins*, by losing much of their religious character at least on the surface of the show, are turned into more universally valid *wrongs*. In my conclusion, I will offer possible explanations for the show's nearly complete abandonment of Bible-based argumentation in favor of worldly messages and emotional effect.

"Queers get AIDS – not me!"

The episode in question starts out with a scene in which a frantic Jonathan breaks the news of his HIV-positive status to Doug. As part of his emotional opening monologue, Jonathan establishes one of the main themes of the episode early on, as he screams out, "It isn't fair, man. Queers get AIDS – not me!" By using the word *queers* in an unmistakably derogatory sense, Jonathan's attitude here constitutes a first hint at an all too frequent feature of evangelical media – the demonization of lesbians and gays (Hendershot, 2004: 12). This can be observed again in a later scene, when Clarence tells Doug about Ty's bisexuality. After both Doug and Clarence repeatedly use the word *queer* in a derogatory sense, Doug shouts out, "Ty, the guy on our track team? The guy that we're in the locker room with? The guy that we shower with all the time?" With this, Doug and Clarence stare at each other, scream out as if in pain, and then turn away from each other in disgust. And later in the episode, Doug calls Ty "sick" after the latter has admitted to having "made a pass" at Clarence.

Considering that this kind of behavior is displayed by two of the show's characters that are perceived as positive, one can only conclude that the intention here is to promote Doug and Clarence's attitude to the show's young audience. This fits Hendershot's insight that Christian abstinence movements regularly attempt to restore teen boys' masculinity through aggressive homophobia (2002: 90). The show's role models Doug and Clarence, who are both virgins, encourage teen boys to mimic their approach to overcome feelings of emasculation.

As illustrated by Jonathan's outcry in the opening scene, *Family First* relies heavily on the specter of AIDS in demonizing homosexuals and gay men in particular, and the implication is that "the point of emergence of the virus should be identified as its *cause*" (Watney, 204). This becomes especially obvious in a scene toward the end of the episode, in which Doug and Clarence confront Ty, who is at a bowling alley with Doug's ex-girlfriend Cheryl. Before the issue of AIDS is even addressed here, Ty is already introduced to the viewer as a sexually and physically aggressive character.

As he walks past an intimidated Clarence, Ty strokes the latter's chin and appears to be taking amused satisfaction in his disgusted reaction. This sexual aggressiveness is echoed twice after Ty is asked outside by Doug to speak in private. Here, Ty admits that "I like sex" before sarcastically mocking Doug by saying, "Listen! Sex is sex. But I guess you wouldn't know much about that, would you?" In addition to being characterized as sexually driven, Ty also comes across as being extremely mean-spirited, as he appears curiously keen on fighting the show's protagonist physically when the two first step out of the building. Then, after finding out that Doug's friend Jonathan was infected with AIDS by Susan, Ty admits to having infected Susan on purpose. When Doug complains that "you're just going around, giving everyone you know AIDS, and you just don't give a rip," Ty responds by saying, "Listen! The more people that get it, the faster they'll come up with a cure! [. . .] Besides, I can't help it – I love them all."

The message here is clear. Men engaging in homosexual activity are sexually aggressive, mean-spirited and indifferent toward other people's feelings. They are responsible for AIDS and are deliberately trying to infiltrate the innocent rest of society with the virus. Accordingly, they do not deserve being treated as victims, their pain is denied acknowledgement. This is an all too familiar observation, as many religious conservatives immediately started representing AIDS as "divine and just retribution for immoral sexual behavior" once the high-risk groups had been identified (Chris Bull and John Gallagher cited in Rimmerman, 132f.). This is mirrored in *Family First*, when the analyzed episode ends with a scene in a room mostly covered in darkness. The viewer witnesses Jonathan's slow, painful death in a hospital bed, accompanied by a sentimental piano tune. Doug is with his friend. He is standing next to the bed, comforting Jonathan in these, his final, moments. Significantly, the audience is supposed to pity the heterosexual character that had pre-marital sex with the girl he loved and wanted to marry (a relatively minor wrong/sin compared to homosexuality). After all, Ty might have been in the hospital bed instead, but this, of course, would not fit the point the show is trying to make. Those who voluntarily engage in homosexual activity are not worthy of pity.

So far, we have seen that homosexual activity and those engaging in it are rejected by *Family First*, and so is pre-marital sex. The justifications offered in the analyzed episode have been purely "secular" in nature. No passages from the Bible have been quoted or referred to indirectly, God has not been mentioned at all.

"I know you made the right choice"

Meanwhile, the second plot line, which introduces pregnancy and abortion as additional issues, emerges in the episode's second scene. Here, Doug's sister, Connie, calls her pregnant friend Amy on the phone to congratulate her, as she is under the false impression that Amy has decided against an abortion. What is particularly interesting in this scene is the way the lighting is used. While Connie, with her mother standing by, is in a brightly lit living-room, the room in which Amy is sitting is dark and gloomy. Then, as Amy is handed the receiver by her mother, the latter acts in a curiously cold way – considering her daughter's weak emotional state – when she says, "Amy, it's for you. And don't talk long!" And only a few moments into the phone call, she orders her daughter to "get off the phone – now!" Clearly, the purpose of the lighting here is to associate abortion with emotional darkness, while having a baby is portrayed as the "enlightened" decision. Also the character of Amy's mother serves to make abortion appear as something threatening that one would not voluntarily opt for. This is further underlined by Connie, who tells her friend, "Listen, I know you made the right choice. That little baby inside you is so precious to God. And I know that when you see that little boy or girl, it'll be all worthwhile."

While the explicit reference to "God" seems to constitute one of the rare exceptions to my thesis of His absence in the series, it is important to note here that the overt religious reference is immediately followed up with a "secular" reason – namely the alleged joys of motherhood. And once again, no Bible passage or other religious grounding is given. A similar observation can be made later in the episode, when Doug and Clarence confront Ty at the bowling alley. First, Doug says to Clarence that "someone needs to tell Ty to get his act together. Maybe God will forgive him." Then outside, the show's protagonist addresses Ty directly telling him that "if you change the way you live, Christ could forgive you, man." Again, the references to God and Christ only constitute brief interruptions in an otherwise strictly "secular" argumentation in which, needless to say, the Bible is not mentioned.

Coming back to the issue of pre-marital sex, Connie's mother explicitly states her opinion after her daughter has hung up the phone in the scene discussed earlier. "I just wish she would have made the right choice three months ago," she says about Amy, and Connie laments, "Why did she go and get pregnant?" A few moments later, Mrs. Collins reminds her daughter that "you won't ever make that mistake, though, Connie. Because you know that you're not ready for that kind of a relationship until after you're married." So, even though Connie has just hinted at religion being a driving force in the family's moral values, her mother now takes the argumentation back to a more neutral level. Instead of following up with a clear reference to "God's will" or a Bible quote, she claims that Connie, as a person, is not ready for sex. Overall, of course, the message implied in the scene involving Connie, Amy and the two mothers is quite clear. Pre-marital sex may result in teen-pregnancy, which, in turn, will bring about the temptation of committing another sin/wrong – namely abortion. The religious reasoning becomes almost imperceptible.

In its promotion of abstinence, *Family First* shows a common feature of Christian fundamentalist media directed at youth – the portrayal of boys as being in a constant battle with their sexual urges (Hendershot, 2002: 92). While the bisexual Ty is the only character who carelessly gives in to his urges, the episode still warns female viewers to regard all boys as potentially dangerous, as certain situations may cause them to lose control over themselves. For example, when Clarence comes to the Collins' house to tell Doug about Ty's sexual advances, he feels that his masculinity has been questioned. Thus, he is constantly lifting a weight he has brought with him and, with Connie in the room, says to her mother, "You know, Mrs. Collins – I like girls." Upon this, the addressed prompts her daughter to accompany her to the garage "where we'll be safe until Clarence leaves." The theme of potentially dangerous male sexuality is echoed again toward the end of the episode, when Doug is told by his ex-girlfriend Cheryl that she was raped by a drunken boy while out of town.

Yet, abortion is the primary focus of the scene immediately following Doug and Clarence's conversation about Ty and AIDS. In this scene, a sad-looking Connie is sitting on a stretcher in a small, dimly lit room, together with her mother and what appears to be a female nurse. Medical equipment in the room leaves no doubt that this is where the abortion is to be performed. Then, as Connie drinks from a small plastic cup, a second moving picture is blended with the primary one. The viewer now continues to see Connie, while in the second picture the camera moves from left to right, showing several content-looking babies lined up in a row. After briefly disappearing, the second picture soon blends with the primary picture again. This time, the camera has zoomed in on one of the babies' faces and it again moves from left to right.

From the beginning of the scene, all this is acoustically accompanied by "Who Will," a highly explicit anti-abortion song recorded by DeGarmo and Key in 1989. Significantly, while DeGarmo and Key were a Christian music group, the song contains only one direct reference to a higher being – namely in the very first line: "It's in His Image they're created." After that, the song abandons even the slightest additional hint at its religious motivation, instead aiming at emotional effect through such passages as, "They long for life with every heartbeat / They speak with tiny hands and feet / But who will help our nation hear them? / It is up to you, it is up to me." Thus, in its strategy, the song directly mirrors the scene in which it appears, as it makes no references to the Bible and only hints at its religious motivation once.

The TV series' scene's over-all purpose – namely to arouse viewers' emotion – becomes especially obvious in its climax. After the happy babies blend with the primary picture for a third time, they disappear again for the primary picture to blend with Amy and her mother discussing Connie's pregnancy in the earlier scene. Shortly after, heavy percussion beats from the song are heard, upon which the camera switches from Amy to three fast cuts that briefly show three images of what appear to be body parts of a dead fetus, two fetuses floating in a reddish liquid and the close-up of a (possibly dead) fetus, respectively. After this, Amy finally demonstrates the kind of reaction this emotionally appealing scene hopes to provoke among the show's viewers. She runs out of the room and decides to keep the baby. Like her, teenage viewers are supposed to take responsibility and actively decide against the evil that is abortion.

Conclusion

As my analysis has shown, *Family First* clearly serves as a Christian fundamentalist tool in that it promotes a number of characteristic moral values. Firstly, the show condemns homosexual activity and demonizes those who engage in it. Aggressive rejection of male homosexuals, in particular, is suggested by the show as a means for sexually abstinent male teens to restore their masculinity. This is partly justified through portraying gays and bisexual men as sexually driven, mean-spirited and physically aggressive. They are identified as the cause of AIDS and are accused of deliberately spreading the virus among the heterosexual majority. In close connection to this, secondly, pre-marital sex is rejected – not only because it is "wrong" but especially because it may lead to infection. In addition, it may lead to teen pregnancy, which is portrayed as highly undesirable. And while sex is generally discussed as something teenagers are simply not ready for, the show warns girls of boys' allegedly dangerous sexual urges. Pregnancy out of wedlock, on the other hand, brings about the confrontation with abortion. This is rejected mainly for ethical reasons such as the innocent child's desire and right to live and is the third point the show intends to make.

In promoting their moral values, the makers of *Family First* rely predominantly on messages that are only ambiguously religious and, in addition, on emotionally effective imagery and music. Religious remarks are few throughout the episode, and there are virtually no references to the Bible. A possible explanation of the show's focus on arousing emotion is offered by Bruce David Forbes, who argues that the move from a "print-dominated age to the Age of Television [...] shifts us to an image-based culture that features explosions of images, fragmented rather than coherent, emphasizing sensation and feeling rather than rationality" (13). I would respond, however, that this is only part of the explanation. While moving pictures (and with them, as in this case, music) are certainly better suited to arouse emotion than, say, a pamphlet, this certainly does not mean that an intellectual argumentation is out of the question or should not be preferred. Thus, the makers of *Family First* employ an emotion-centered strategy *not* because they have no choice, but because they sense that, in connection with moving images, it is the most promising way of manipulating the show's young viewers (Hoover 158). As Hendershot points out, "today's conservative evangelicals want to engage with the wider culture because they think their belief system is the truth – indeed, the only hope for humankind – and they want to share this reality with others" (2004: 11). In trying to do so, *Family First* deliberately keeps its religious messages subtle so as not to "scare off" anyone from outside the underlying belief system. What appears to have become of sole importance is *that* certain religious values prevail in the general population. That they prevail *for religious reasons* appears almost entirely insignificant in the context of the show.

Of course, as I have pointed out in my analysis, the episode at hand is not free of references to a higher being, which is in fact the only explicit indication that the values promoted are religiously motivated. However, the allusions to God are put in only for the benefit of the show's regular base of viewers from a Christian fundamentalist background. The religious references are exclusively made in the form of side remarks, brief and casual enough to be by-passed comfortably by those who do not embrace them as truth. In essence, then, *Family First* is designed very carefully so as to have mass appeal – through "secular" argumentations and emotionally effective images and music – while at the same time maintaining its appeal to Christian fundamentalists.

Works Cited

Abelove, Henry, Michèle Aina Barale and David M. Halperin, eds. *The Lesbian and Gay Studies Reader*. New York: Routledge, 1993. Print.

Browning, Don S. et al. *Religion and the American Family Debate: From Culture Wars to Common Ground*. Louisville: Westminster John Knox, 2000. Print.

"Family First." *Fire by Nite*. Willie George Ministries Television Studio. Church on the Move, Tulsa. 1986-1992. Television.

Forbes, Bruce David and Jeffrey H. Mahan, eds. *Religion and Popular Culture in America*. Berkeley: U of California P, 2000. Print.

Forbes, Bruce David. "Introduction: Finding Religion in Unexpected Places." *Religion and Popular Culture in America*. Eds. Bruce David Forbes and Jeffrey H. Mahan. Berkeley: U of California P, 2000. 1-20. Print.

Hendershot, Heather. "Holiness Codes and Holy Homosexuals: Interpreting Gay and Lesbian Christian Subculture." *Camera Obscura* 45 (2000): 151-93. Print.

Hendershot, Heather. "Virgins for Jesus: The Gender Politics of Therapeutic Christian Fundamentalist Media." *Hop on Pop: The Politics and Pleasures of Popular Culture*. Eds. Henry Jenkins, Tara McPherson and Jane Shattuc. Durham: Duke UP, 2002. 88-104. Print.

Hendershot, Heather. *Shaking the World for Jesus: Media and Conservative Evangelical Culture*. Chicago: U of Chicago P, 2004. Print.

Hoover, Stewart M. "Visual Religion in Media Culture." *The Visual Culture of American Religion*. Eds. David Morgan and Sally M. Promey. Berkeley: U of California P, 2001. 146-59. Print.

Jenkins, Henry, Tara McPherson and Jane Shattuc, eds. *Hop on Pop: The Politics and Pleasures of Popular Culture*. Durham: Duke UP, 2002. Print.

Morgan, David and Sally M. Promey, eds. *The Visual Culture of American Religion*. Berkeley: U of California P, 2001. Print.

Rimmerman, Craig A. *From Identity to Politics: The Lesbian and Gay Movements in the United States*. Philadelphia: Temple UP, 2002. Print.

Watney, Simon. "The Spectacle of AIDS." *The Lesbian and Gay Studies Reader*. Eds. Henry Abelove, Michèle Aina Barale and David M. Halperin. New York: Routledge, 1993. 202-11. Print.

'Death Becomes Her': Representations of Death, Afterlife and God in American TV-Series

Christian Lenz

Death marks the distinct end. Or does it? 84% of Americans according to "The Harris Poll – The Religious and Other Beliefs of Americans 2003" believe that their souls will survive and experience a transition into a new, other form of life – an afterlife. In my essay I will explore the notions and connections of death, the afterlife and the function of God with respect to them as they are represented in American mainstream television. Furthermore, I will concentrate on the question of how popular secular, or maybe 'post-secular' (Habermas) television uses and challenges conventional Christian faith and its inherent power structures. In my analysis I will focus on the TV-series *Dead Like Me*, which aired from 2003 to 2004. I will start with a very short introduction to the historic sources that color the representation of death and the afterlife up to today.

From the beginning of peoples' histories, humans have wondered what comes after death. The Egyptians have, similar to the Romans and Greeks, developed the idea of a second empire, a land which can only be entered once one has drawn one's last breath. It is generally believed in all old religions that the afterlife has a magnificent place at the ready, which is a place of pleasure and eternal joy. The Greeks called this place "Elysium" and Christians today designate it 'heaven.' The idea of a paradisiacal place was derived from ancient Persia and has been adapted by people of Jewish and later on, Christian faiths. It is the Greek translation of the 'Garden of Eden,' which has entered English via Latin "paradises" and French "paradis" (McKean). Paradise is reserved for the good and faithful who live happily ever after – although it has to be admitted that Christian belief traces the original sin to Adam and Eve's lapse in Paradise, and thus it also has a negative connotation. While Adam and Eve were "sent ... forth from the garden of Eden, to till the ground from whence [they were] taken," (Genesis 3:23), the dark counterpart of Paradise for the people who have not behaved according to the rules their society has set up is hell – at least in Biblical terms. Greek and Roman mythology referred to it as "Tartaros," the negative counterpart to the Elysium in Hades. In Norse mythology, "Hel" was actually the name given to "the place where the dead are, [...] and it seems to signify the place of the dead in general rather than any one place of the dead in particular" (Ellis 84).

Fast forward a few hundred years and welcome to the second millennium. Greek,

Roman and Teutonic belief systems have long been gone and replaced by Christianity, Islam or Buddhism, to name but the most popular ones. If we turn to America, there is an abundance of faiths, and people can adhere to any religion they want. Many of them turn especially to Christianity, (to which I will refer from now on as it is the ultimate context of the TV show I will discuss), which embraces the belief in eternal life and founds its faith on the idea that wo/man's life on earth is merely a stop before s/he enters another stage. This other, post-mortem stage can be thought to take place in heaven or, maybe, hell. Whereas in earlier times, heaven was thought to be a place where one could gain eternal life and would be compensated for earlier shortcomings, e.g. poverty or any other afflictions (*Religion in Geschichte und Gegenwart* 1760), today it has become more and more 'up for grabs' with regard to the expectations of what might be waiting for the deceased. But just as challenging as the positive image of the afterlife in heaven, is the notion of its negative counterpart – hell. For who would like to end up in a place where s/he is to endure everlasting torture? Thus, death and the afterlife have always been invaluable instruments of power for religious leaders, and they still are today. The aforementioned Harris Poll has found that 82% of Americans believe in heaven and 69% in hell. Moreover, the interviewed Christians were apparently very sure of themselves as 75% think they will rise up to heaven once they pass away, whereas only 1% are adamant that they will go to hell.

Looking back on a long tradition of death and "entertainment" – the oldest form being the *Totentanz* (Dance of Death) in the middle of the 14th century (Herbermann and Williamson) – popular TV has re-discovered religious topics in this 'post-secular' age. In TV series like, e.g., *This is the Life*, *Insight* or *Highway to Heaven*, which all have distinct religious motifs and motivations, death and the afterlife are reinterpreted for a mass audience. Thereby TV joins other forces (and media) in modifying an interpretive power that had been wielded primarily by the church(es) for a long time. Whether the effect of this re-interpretation is revolutionary and liberating, repetitive and conservative or both is a question to be grappled with on the next pages.

Dead Like Me is an interesting case in the re-envisioning of death today. It focuses on young Georgia "George" Lass, who is killed by a flaming toilet seat in the very first episode. In her afterlife – which incidentally is taking place in the same city she used to live in – she becomes a grim reaper and her job is to collect souls from other people's bodies. The reason for her new job is a simple regulation: Every reaper has a quota of souls to collect. Once this quota is met, the former reaper hands the duties over to his/her last "customer" and moves on (to a place that is a mystery that is never addressed). George was the one to inherit the job from the former reaper (the why is as mysterious as the whereabouts of her predecessor). To add insult to injury, George has to serve "customers" whilst entertaining a day job – reapers do not get paid – and keeping her grip on 'life.' When she is first presented to the audience, it becomes clear very quickly that as long as she was alive she was a woman without any 'life' at all: She had no friends, no job, no perspective and hardly any incentive to change her miseries. She was 'dead' whilst living. The lethal toilet seat, which catapults her to the hereafter, starts her 'real' life – and it is not pure chance that the seat comes from above: literally "from above" because it is a part of the abandoned Russian space station Mir, and metaphorically "from above" as a glaring hint that she has been chosen for a career in the afterlife. As heaven 'above' has – contrary to hell 'beneath' – always been considered to be the sphere of God, the toilet seat is, supposedly, God-sent. It seems that it was only her body which kept her on the 'wrong' side of death and she has now been 'redeemed.'

Although George did not believe in Christianity, the series suggests that she longed to do so, because she would have liked to pray to God to change her miserable status on earth. Yet, while still alive, God fell into the same category as Santa Claus, the Easter Bunny or the Tooth-Fairy for her. The heroine's disbelief already points to the problems and issues George and many other characters in the series have with God. He has been banned to the same fairy-tale existence as the creatures used to soothe small children. But general disbelief in his existence is not God's only problem in the series, as can be seen in the opening of the pilot episode.

In this episode, George as omniscient voice-over narrator, tells the audience how death came into the world. According to her story, god handed over the urn of death to a toad who then broke it. This account suggests that god was an overworked, somewhat conniving being. He unloads his own duty of caring about and guarding death unto an amphibian – thus having found a scapegoat, or "god's fall guy on the whole death issue," as George puts it in the show. Thereby god is not to be blamed for the fact that people die, because it was the toad who did not perform his duty of guarding the urn properly. The fact that god is not prepared to take full responsibility leads the whole moral binary of right and wrong into a crisis. He knowingly flaunts his own rules of always being right and a role model. The series suggests that god is less interested in earth's inhabitants than the Bible propagates. If God used to be the ultimate locus of power, not to be got by or above, *Dead Like Me* strips away this power and releases god from his position as the final judge over and mover of all beings.

From the way George tells it, one can assume that she has acquired insider knowledge and thus we have to believe her that 'God' exists but is spelled with a lower case "g" instead of an upper case one (This essay will maintain the spelling as suggested by George: Thus, it is "God" in the Christian sense and "god" when I work with *Dead Like Me*'s definition). George's report shows that He has not the position of the Almighty anymore but rather the status of 'some' creator. Interestingly enough, George's introductory story strongly suggests that she has insider knowledge of god's existence but shortly after she has become a reaper and inquires after God, she is denied any affirmative response as to his presence. This refusal will be maintained throughout the whole series. God's paradoxical status of existing whilst being absent will be discussed below.

This leads us to the rendering of death itself. Depictions of death have been made for ages and the most popular image today shows a skeleton clothed in a shroud with scythe and hourglass – although very recently even Brad Pitt impersonated the Grim Reaper in *Meeting Joe Black* (1998), his youthful, beautiful body in a tuxedo testifying to death's many different visualizations today. In these and other representations, death has been rendered 'visible' and was thus potentially de-demonized for humans in order not to be afraid. Visualizations and, in particular, personifications of death as grim skeletal, or able-bodied reaper help to come to terms with the finality of life: They might even make humans feel equal, if not superior to the inevitable end. The banning of invisible death into a visual system leads us to believe that we have power over death, which in truth we have not. What we can look at and see is not as frightening as something we cannot see. And people prefer death looking like Brad Pitt rather than hovering about them as an incomprehensible and uncanny 'nonbeing.' Along the same lines, Garret Stewart has stated that death is "a motif without referent" (4) which has to be filled up every time anew.

Yet, in *Dead Like Me*, death is normalized, and thus de-demonized in even more dramatically entertaining ways. It is not just a skeleton, or Brad Pitt for that matter, but many different people working as grim reapers. Moreover, we are told that this is a job just like any other. The only real difference is that one is chosen – without ever applying – for the job and has to be dead before taking up the duty. Betty, another dead woman in the series, smilingly proclaims that becoming a reaper is "a destiny thing." Personal choice is thus still eliminated – death's job is providence in its purest form. After having died, one first becomes un-dead and subsequently a grim reaper. Hence, a second career might await one after one's death. One can even be promoted from a grim reaper but it is not explicitly stated what to. Here, the spiritualist notion of 'evolving' is taken into account and mixed with Christian mythology. One might become an angel, of which Rube, the chief grim reaper, says that they "don't like getting their hands dirty – [...] upper-management types." The sweet hereafter appears to be structured like an apposite business with managers or administrators (angels), executives (reapers) and customers (the soon to be deceased). The question remains: Who is the boss of everything and everybody? Can it still be god, the one who made a toad a scapegoat because he did not want to be in charge of something as important as death? The answer to this riddle is not even addressed within the series, although George asks directly if God exists – but gets no answer to that either. Her voice-over in the opening sequence suggests that he does exist but is a rather lousy business man who does not take on responsibilities and therefore is not one to be head of angels and reapers. Still, the series is built on the notion that the greatest power man can think of is the control of death.

The Christian Church as institution claims that this power lies in God's hands alone for He already resurrected Jesus Christ from the dead and only He can grant eternal 'after-life.' As Michel Foucault argues in *The History of Sexuality*, the Church works like a repressive machinery (81) and thus "acts in a uniform and comprehensive manner; it operates according to the simple and endlessly reproduced mechanisms of law [and] taboo" (84). These mechanisms are inscribed in the Bible, for instance, in the Biblical command "Depart from me, you accursed, into the eternal fire that has been prepared for the devil and his angels," and in the subsequent description of the command's effects in that they "will depart into eternal punishment, but the righteous into eternal life" (Matthew 25, 41 & 46). These passages suggest that people who do not live according to Biblical laws will descend to hell after they have passed away. Only true Christians may rise to heaven. This enforces both law – do live according to God's principles if you want to go to heaven – and taboo – thou shalt not dare to not live according to the principles laid down in the Scripture. The Christian Church, which interprets and teaches the Bible, is the machinery which executes the power which is said to be 'God's.'

Therefore, Christianity has produced an axis of power that rises from the faithful believer (who is more powerful than non-believers) to the apostles or evangelists (who were/are closer to God and thus announce His word) to God Himself (who wields the power over His flock). Depending on the different denominations, there might be many levels of power in between, e.g., in Catholicism where they reach from the common church goer (who is positioned above the ones outside his church), over priests and bishops (who are more powerful than the common believer) to the pope (who is even more powerful because he is the direct deputy of God on earth) and finally God. The only problem is that God, contrary to every other constituent of the axis of power, is not present on earth and 'speaks' to His followers only through the mouths and writings of His deputies. The people who are interested in maintaining this axis of power reinforce the belief that God were represented by human deputies although there is no proof that the latter were appointed, or their words were authorized by God. Yet as there is no other access to God and it is a sin to accuse spiritual leaders or Scripture of not announcing God's word, the power has shifted from a mighty creator to fallible mortals and their interpretable texts. God has no direct access to his followers, he is more or less cut off from his own axis: He is only said to be existing but remains forever absent.

In *Dead Like Me* this situation is mirrored but blatantly highlighted in the funny plot. The locus of power over death is even less tangible than in traditional Christian thought and Church practices, as god seems to have lost any direct grip on power and through George the audience learns that grim reapers, far from being self-determined, only do what they are told to do. Grim reapers are assigned to special divisions for deaths. Her division is "'External Influence.' Translation: murders, suicides, accidents and et cetera" (George). The other divisions would be dealing with 'normal' deaths, like illnesses or dying of old age, that is deaths of people who have reached the 'natural' end of their life spans, no interfering necessary. With the "external influence," there are two options. Either people end other people's life via murder, or Gravelings – gruesome creatures that are part of the hereafter – "set things in motion" (Rube) which cause the death of a human being. For example they cut a rope so that an apparently securely tied up piano lands on a woman. Still, they do not kill people, they merely set the stage. So where is the locus of power over death? It is within the axis of 'celestial business' as I would like to call it.

I already mentioned that the hereafter is structured like a company with angels, reapers and customers. All reapers get the names, places and "Estimated Time[s] of Death" (Mason) each morning for the souls to collect on that day. So people's deaths are planned even before their last day has arrived. Rube, "External Influence's" chief, has a diary which holds all appointments of reapers with their customers. Also, Mason, one of George's fellow reapers, remarks that "some reapers believe your appointment with death is on their books before you're even born." This again would support the explanation of death by providence. However, one cannot call the angels' careful planning 'providence' because that would be God's overall plan. And *Dead Like Me*'s opening has not characterized god as the being to make important choices. Again, god as the ultimate locus of power is bracketed; the decision about death has been relocated from god to the managers of his company. Interestingly enough, *Dead Like Me* thereby mirrors the axis of power established by Christian denominations, as described above. It employs the same notion of the actual existence of an axis with god on top and places the audience and George (as common believers/executives) at the other end, eager to find out about the way it functions and who is in control. And just like the common believers they are denied any conclusive answer or information by the text itself. They are given only interpretations which can vary immensely from interpreter to interpreter.

Thus, the series strikingly suggests that god has become a mere Baudrillardian simulacrum of the third order, which masks the absence of a reliable reality. The sign 'death' (Stewart), although visualized by multiple and potentially unthreatening grim reapers, is bound up with a certain axis of power which has its locus and foundation not in a superior being but is managed 'somehow' by administrators. As a result 'death' in *Dead Like Me* – contrary to its Christian model – points to a potential absence of the highest being, or rather it does not affirm its presence. A hyperreal obfuscation is created which only refers to other signs but never to any 'real' content: god is lost in a blurring mist of signs. Although *Dead Like Me* apparently confirms His existence through George's narrative, and despite the staging of Angels and other creatures populating Heaven, it never allows him to appear and shifts his duties to other departments on the celestial axis. This absence from a stage that merrily visualizes whatever else was thought to populate Heaven, marks H/him as 'dead' or, maybe even worse, inevitably useless. God has become a harmless myth that turns around his own redundancy. While the power over/of death remains a mysterious "motif without referent," which keeps the series going, God has been turned into "a motif without referent" that needs no further speculation.

While in real-life the Christian organization of social life works with machinations that hide that G/god is ultimately not 'there' in order to establish H/his presence (Barthes 141), *Dead Like Me* has taken up the notion of the Christian God's absence and illustrates it with a set of characters, celestial helpers that stand in for god. In order to do so, the writers of the script had to find a reason for god's absence and found it in his unwillingness to take the reins. The TV show points towards the fact that god is absent and, obviously, that there is no need to fill the gap. This suggests that although 'God' and 'death' are still in usage as Christian signifiers, it is the latter which keeps its power up to now, whereas the former needn't be filled with any meaning anymore. It does not make any difference whether G/god exists (within or outside of *Dead Like Me*) or not. He handed over the urn of death to the toad and withdrew completely into otiosity.

It is not only *Dead Like Me* which utilizes, changes, subverts and, to a certain extent criticizes traditional, and in particular Christian notions of heaven, hell and the afterlife in its plots and fictitious settings. The TV-series *Desperate Housewives*, which depicts the lives of various female characters in an American suburb, for instance, is even bolder in its rendering of heaven and hell. The pilot episode presents Mary Alice, one of the central group of girl friends, who lives through a normal morning which has her "quietly polishing the routine of [her] life until it gleamed with perfection" (Mary Alice's voice-over), only to finally shoot herself. In Christian terms, her suicide is a big sin against God – who gave mankind free will but forbade them to end their own life. Moreover, she has also killed another human being – which is a violation of the Commandment "Thou shalt not kill." Thus she should not be allowed to go to heaven. But Mary Alice's voice-over narration implies that she is at no unpleasant place at all, thereby ruling out purgatory and hell. The state she finds herself in grants her complete knowledge of everybody's lives and secrets and even allows her to foresee the future – a very good afterlife for a murderess who committed suicide, indeed. Christianity's function of control over people would be extremely diminished if believers took to the notion that crimes might be punished by society *but* the hereafter erased one's sins and welcomed one with the gift of eternal wisdom and pleasantness.

If one thinks of the series *Charmed* – which is located in supernatural fantasy world – yet another view is opened up. While the various forms of evil in *Charmed* – following traditional belief – usually stem from the underworld and the show locates the benign power in heaven, it is populated by a group of powerful former witches who possess eternal wisdom. While witches would usually have resided in hell, here they are positively connoted and placed in the above.

While in both these series, earth has become a quasi-Biblical battlefield for heaven and hell with (extraordinary) humans in the middle and a very conventional vertical axis of bad (beneath) and good (above) is created, the inhabitants of heaven are pretty unconventional. Thereby the two tv-series, just like *Dead Like Me*, illustrate a strong trend in American TV-culture. They play with religious ideas and traditions in order to challenge – or sometimes to support – theistic concepts in order to create new varieties of entertainment.

The analysis has shown that religious belief systems have come a long way since the days of the Egyptians or Romans. Today, people are offered a whole variety of versions of how death, afterlife and the supposedly mighty being behind it all work. *Dead Like Me* fares quite heretically with religion as such and it points towards interesting questions, even if they cannot be answered by the series. Yet it still presents the audience with a kind of Christian version of life and death. It constructs an axis of deputy power related to the one structuring Christian faith and its social practice and with its narrative about god's toad, it opens itself to subversive hints toward God's absence as well as traditional readings of god's temporary withdrawal.

Other shows like *Desperate Housewives* have been even more idiosyncratic in their construction of the afterlife. But, as in *Dead Like Me*, we can only guess its configuration as the audience never gets to see it. However, series that take up and challenge parts of Christian faith and introduce obvious fantasy elements into what is still recognizable as a basically Christian universe might raise the awareness of the function of this religion and the ideology that stands behind it. They point to the fact that in our 'post-secular' age, a turn to religious configurations of death and the thereafter might be less an expression of a religious revival but more of a further erosion of the locus of power in the established churches, a shift of the axis of control from religion to popular television or culture in general. Let us pray for that.

Works Cited

Barthes, Roland. *S/Z*. Trans. Richard Miller. New York: Hill and Wang, 1974. Print.

Baudrillard, Jean. "From The Precession of Simulacra." *Norton Anthology of Theory and Criticism*. Ed. Vincent B. Leitch. New York: Norton, 2001. 1732-41. Print.

Ellis, Hilda Roderick. *The Road to Hell. A Study of the Conception of the Dead in Old Norse Literature*. Cambridge: UP, 1943. Print.

Foucault, Michel. *The History of Sexuality: An Introduction*. Vol I. New York: Vintage Books, 1990. Print.

Goodwin, Sarah Webster, and Elisabeth Bronfen. Introduction. *Death and Representations*. Eds. Sarah Webster Goodwin and Elisabeth Bronfen. London: The Johns Hopkins UP, 1993. 3-25. Print.

Habermas, Jürgen. "Notes on a Post-Secular Society." *Signandsight.com*. Signandsight, 18 Jun. 2008. Web. 4 May 2010.

Herbermann, Charles, and George Williamson. "Dance of Death." *The Catholic Encyclopedia*. Vol. 4. New York: Robert Appleton Company. 23 Mar. 2009. Web. 4 May 2010.

McKean, Erin, ed. *The New Oxford American Dictionary*. 2nd ed. Oxford: Oxford UP, 2005. Print.

"Pilot." *Dead Like Me*. Showtime. 27 Jun. 2003. Television.

"Pilot." *Desperate Housewives*. ABC. 3 Oct. 2004. Television.

Religion in Geschichte und Gegenwart. Handwörterbuch für Theologie und Religionswissenschaft. Vol 2. Tübingen, 1998. Print.

Rose, Jacqueline, and Juliet Mitchell, eds. *Feminine Sexuality: Jacques Lacan and the école freudienne*. New York: Norton, 1985. Print.

Stewart, Garrett. *Death Sentences: Styles of Dying in British Fiction*. Cambridge: Harvard UP, 1984. Print.

Taylor, Humphrey. "The Religious and Other Beliefs of Americans 2003." *The Harris Poll*. Harris Interactive. 29 Jun. 2007. Web. 4 May 2010.

United States. Bureau of Justice Statistics. *Homicide Trends in the U.S.: Most Victims and Perpetrators in Homicides are Male*. Bureau of Justice Statistics. 23 Mar. 2009. Web. 4 May 2010.

Religion in *Lost*: Managing a National Crisis on U.S. Television

Maria Verena Siebert

This analysis will shed light on the representation of religion in American popular culture by taking a closer look at the first two seasons of one of the most popular U.S. TV shows of the last years: *Lost*. The basic premise of the mystery-drama-series (2004-2010) is that of a classical robinsonade: A group of strangers is stranded on a tropical island after a plane crash. They have to master survival in the wilderness and fight the mysterious, only seemingly primitive "Others" and "The Monster," not knowing whether or not they have been exposed to "The Virus." In a parallel plot line, each episode focuses on the past of one character and follows how s/he develops for the better on the island.

Though references to particular church-based belief systems are only made in single episodes and therein only in plot lines focusing on minor characters and their private religious practices, another dimension of religion permeates the major plot line of the entire show. This paper will show that a conservative version of American civil religion and its unifying function for American national identity are central to the message of *Lost*. The analysis will be based on an understanding of civil religion in America as outlined by Robert N. Bellah in his famous 1967 article by the same title. Bellah analyzes the political rhetoric of John F. Kennedy, Abraham Lincoln and George Washington to investigate the particular features of a "religious dimension," as he calls it, that is "well-institutionalized" in America and yet "clearly differentiated from the churches" (168). What becomes clear in Bellah's analysis is that, whereas private religious beliefs may vary, it is the function of civil religion to create unity and consensus among Americans by focusing on a number of basic religious concepts that are shared by people of various denominations. For Bellah this is basically a positive dimension, though he is aware that "civil religion has not always been evoked in favor of worthy causes" (181f) and that it is historically contingent.

The analysis of *Lost* will trace its references to religion from the private to the civil dimension of its religious discourse. In a first step, it will be shown how religion is used to support and illustrate the storyline in the episodes focusing on the characterization of two Catholic characters in season two of the series. Catholicism, as associated with these characters, is the only institutionalized religion whose private dimension is explored in the series, although the ensemble of characters constitutes itself from

73

a variety of national, ethnic and social backgrounds, suggesting a greater variety of religious denominations.

In a second step, *Lost*'s depiction of Catholicism will be contrasted with its approach to American civil religion. While private belief is present in isolated episodes, the representation of civil religion develops throughout the show. A closer look at John Locke, the central character who – probably like most viewers – tries to make meaning from the apparently coincidental experiences on the island, will allow making some of the implicit religious messages of the show explicit.

In the summary, the effect of the interconnection of the representations of both private belief and civil religion in the series will be discussed. Thereby, the role as cultural strategy of crisis management in *Lost* will be revealed.

The Representation of Religion in *Lost*

Lost was part of a trend of large ensemble casts. Reviewer Bill Keveney suggests that the advantage of this phenomenon is that "[l]arge casts can easily present a mix of racial, ethnic and socioeconomic groups." He stresses that "*Lost*'s Sayid (Naveen Andrews), a former member of Iraq's Republican Guard, is a TV regular unlikely to be seen in a show with a small cast." Indeed, with its inclusion of American ethnic minorities (Latin American and African American), and by featuring Korean, Iraqi, Australian, British and Nigerian characters, *Lost* looks like it were in favor of multiculturalism through its representation. However, the fact that the white, male, heterosexual, upper middle-class American physician, Jack Shepherd, is almost immediately expected by all of the survivors of the crash to lead the group and that he, indeed, takes over indicates from the very beginning that *Lost* is a show that naturalizes white, male, heterosexual, upper middle-class American leadership.

The central importance of this character is already suggested by the fact that the exposition, which stages the immediate aftermath of the plane crash, is focalized through him. In the series' second episode, "White Rabbit," he is initially reluctant to play the part everyone expects him to play, but in the denouement, his position as head of the survivors is clear. It is cemented by a speech reminiscent of John Winthrop's sermon "A Model of Christian Charity" for the passengers of the *Arabella:*

[W]ee must be knitt together, in this worke, as one man. Wee must entertaine each other in brotherly affection. Wee must be willing to abridge ourselves of our superfluities, for the supply of other's necessities. [...] Wee must delight in eache other; make other's conditions our oune; rejoice together, mourne together, labour and suffer together, allwayes haueving before our eyes our commission and community in the worke, as members of the same body. (303)

Similarly, Jack also starts his short address to the other survivors by explaining to them that they are in a special situation where they must shed their individual desires and start to think and work as a community if they are to succeed in mastering survival on the island:

Every man for himself is not going to work. It's time to start organizing. We need to figure out how we're going to survive here. Now, I found water. Fresh water, up in the valley. I'll take a group in at first light. If you don't want to go, then find another way to contribute. Last week most of us were strangers. But we're all here now. ("White Rabbit")

Both speakers thus aim to create a community out of the individuals before them. They underline the urgency of their plea by painting a vivid picture of what will happen if their counsel is not heard. Winthrop fears that "if wee shall deale falsely with our God in this work wee haue undertaken [...], [w]ee shall shame the faces of many of God's worthy servants, and cause theire prayers to be turned into curses upon us till wee be consumed out of the good land whither wee are a going" (303). Jack suggests, more curtly, "if we can't live together, we're going to die alone" ("White Rabbit"). Both men feel responsible for the group and its well-being, yet what they understand under the latter term differs. Winthrop is a shepherd in the Christian sense, as he does not only try to keep the "herd" together, but also on the right path, the path to God. Though Jack is not concerned with such spiritual matters but with the imminent survival of the group, through his second name, "Shepherd" we are invited to consider him such. Jack's initial and obvious qualification as hero, his capability to save others and to handle dangerous situations cool-mindedly, which he acquired through his profession as a physician, is consolidated by his willingness and ability to forge a community out of strangers. Thus, the male Anglo-Saxon doctor appears as the natural choice for the job of metaphorical shepherd of this coincidental community. Among the many nationalities stranded on the island, it is someone who represents the traditional hegemonial group in the US who takes center stage in *Lost* and thereby prepares the centering of the plot on American national identity. Analyzing the community of the plane-crash survivors and its identity in opposition to the mysterious "Others" on the island, Michael Newbury also finds that "*Lost* features more a narrative of assimilation than a narrative of multinationalism or transnational affiliation" (206). He explains,

[t]he community of survivors is defined less by global movement than it is by a privileged, even mythological, narrative of multicultural absorption into American nationhood. The point I would like to emphasize, though, is how profoundly *national* this imagined racial community is. (ibid.)

Likewise, *Lost* cannot fulfill its promise of multiculturalism when it comes to religion. Although we catch glimpses of Sayid praying in a mosque or on board a ship, the only religion receiving thorough attention in the first two seasons is Christianity and more accurately the Catholicism of both the Nigerian (Mr.) Eko and the English Charlie Pace. However, Catholicism is repeatedly presented as "other" or exotic. It is instead

American civil religion that is continuously present in the show's overarching plot-line and that emerges as a crucial tool for survival on the island. The representation of American civil religion in *Lost* reaffirms Newbury's thesis of the "privileged [...]] narrative of multicultural absorption into American nationhood" (ibid.) in this TV series, as the following analysis will demonstrate.

Private Religious Belief in *Lost*: Catholicism as Represented by Charlie and Eko

Both Charlie and Eko belong to the numerous minor characters of the cast of *Lost*. Charlie is a young, white, British one-hit-wonder rock star and a drug addict. Eko, a middle-aged, muscle-packed black Nigerian, is a drug-dealer who – up to the plane crash – lived under the guise of being a priest. In the episode "Psalm 23" the stories of these two characters are unravelled, and the unravelling centers in both cases on drugs and religion.

The exploration of the sins of the past of Charlie and Eko offers an abundance of Christian icons, symbols and references and the series uses an abundance of religious symbolism to mark their paths. Whenever they wind up at a crossroad of good and evil, Catholic imagery underlines the importance of the choice to make: When the recovering drug-addicted Charlie is tempted to fall back into old habits, it is by a stash of heroin pouring from a broken Virgin Mary statue ("The 23rd Psalm"). When Charlie makes the decision to abstain from drugs for good, he and Eko burn the heroin while Eko recites a psalm (namely psalm 23, "The Shepherd Psalm") over the fire. When, in a retrospective scene, Eko is picked up as an innocent child by a gang of murderers who will make him one of them, this is marked by a gang member tearing a necklace with the holy cross from Eko's neck ("Fire and Water"). When Eko has atoned for his sins after the plane crash, he finds the necklace on the island and puts it on again. In addition, Eko is shown to carry a piece of wood with engravings of bible quotes wherever he goes. It is dubbed "The Jesus Stick" by Charlie and functions as Eko's reminder of his sins. Charlie himself seems so deeply immersed in Catholic iconography that, when he has one of the typical island visions, which most plane-crash survivors have from time to time, it appears in the style of the biblical paintings of his childhood home ("Fire and Water"). Eko even starts, with the help of Charlie, building a church on the island and he baptizes the baby of atheistic Claire. This is a notable reversal of history – the black Nigerian who landed on an island and becomes the missionary among white Anglo-Saxons who are stranded like him – yet it is presented without a hint of irony. In case the viewer might still be immune to the plethora of religious symbolism, Claire – who seems not to care about religion like the majority of the survivors (including the main characters Jack, John, Kate and

Sawyer) – explicitly points out that Eko and Charlie stand in sharp contrast to the others: "So you are religious, hu?" ("The 23rd Psalm").

Catholic symbolism, then, marks the path of the two fallen men back to what is morally righteous. However, all characters on the island are following this same path, whether they are deeply religious or appear not to be religious at all. Though the show excessively employs Christian markers in the episodes focusing on Charlie and Eko, the general course from sin to atonement is not specific to them. Their moral renewal happens to be ordered in religious terms, but Catholicism is employed as a system of signs that is an heirloom; a belief with an oral and written tradition, with rituals and habits that have a particular history. In the present, it is something displaced from the (American) viewer's reality to such strange places as Europe and Nigeria. Both Eko's and Charlie's experiences tied up with Catholicism are excessively marked as foreign – already in the first shot of their respective homes in Europe and Africa the viewer immediately recognizes, that "We are not in Kansas anymore" without the help of any explanatory captions. The flashback to Eko's childhood in Africa ("Fire and Water") is shot in a warm, red-golden sunlight. We are at a pastoral setting where boys whirl up clouds of dry earth by playing soccer while African women carry baskets on their heads along the road in the background. In contrast, the flashback to Charlie's past in Britain ("The Moth") shows him and his brother in front of a Gothic archway denoting "old Europe." The light is dark, cold and blue. It is obviously very windy and the ground is covered by fallen leaves. Catholicism is thus displaced to these strange and exotic lands, the Third World and the Old World and it is from there that they are imported to the island.

Catholicism as a system of signs is familiar to the viewers even though it is no longer their own, which is why it can be employed by the writers of the show as a code of communication. However, at the same time, it occurs as something strange and exotic in our secularized world – both in the fictional space of the island as well as in the real space in front of the TV set. Thus it is a spectacular system of signs that serves as foreground to what otherwise remains implicit in the rest of the series. Though Catholicism, as represented by Charlie and Eko, is portrayed respectfully and positively in the series, it is distanced from the audience and represented, if not as "other," at least as "off centre." Through the repeated depiction of the spectacular imagery and traditions of their Catholicism, a difference from the rest of the survivors is stressed. Bellah illuminates, with the help of a quotation from Benjamin Franklin's autobiography, the dividing effect of institutionalized religions – religions like Charlie's and Eko's Catholicism in the series – in contrast to the effect of civil religion, which unites across denominational differences:

I was never without some religious principles. I never doubted, for instance, the existence of the Deity; that made the world and govern'd it by his Providence; that the most acceptable service of God was the doing of good to men; that our souls are Immortal; and that all crime will be punished, and virtue rewarded either here or hereafter. These I esteemed the essentials of every religion; and, being to be found in all the religions we had in our country, I respected them all, tho' with different degrees of respect, as I found them more or less mix'd with other articles, which, without any tendency to inspire, promote or confirm morality, serv'd principally do [sic] divide us, and make us unfriendly to one another. (qtd. in Bellah 173)

Franklin identifies a set of dogmas here that he considers essential to every religion: the existence of a benevolent god, the immortality of souls and the reward of virtue versus the punishment of crime. He claims that everything beyond that serves to create difference. Transferred to *Lost* this means that the specific features of Eko's and Charlie's religion that go beyond Franklin's general dogmas estrange them from the rest of the group (as well as many of the viewers). Civil religion in contrast, a system that consists only of Franklin's list of basic beliefs, can create unity in an otherwise disparate group by focusing on what they all are able to agree on. For utilitarian purposes, the religious belief of subjects like Charlie and Eko has a place within the mini-global community of *Lost*'s heroes because it serves their moral development for the better and also serves the welfare of the community. It is, however, not as central to the show as the privileged representation of American civil religion, which is transported through the series' handling of faith and providence, as will be extrapolated in the next part of this paper.

American Civil Religion: Religion and American National Identity

[A] TV show that so persistently focuses on men who need to protect women, while pondering not-so-deep issues like the importance of "faith" (in what?!) leaves me cold. (Hendershot on *Lost*, no pag.)

As Heather Hendershot ironically suggests in the quote above, "faith" is a major topic of *Lost*. The issue is raised again and again by another male American in the show, who is named John Locke. Locke is the character who functions as the key in opening and closing the series' entry way to religion and national identity. He can be read as the prototypical Western hero: the white, male, heterosexual Anglo-Saxon who turns from a domesticated and metaphorically "impotent" paralytic to a "potent" hunter and gatherer while managing survival in the wilderness. Though all survivors transform on the island in one way or another, John Locke most obviously undergoes the prototypical American frontier experience.

In addition to his acquisition of practical survival skills he, who had been mocked and patronized by institutions and other men before landing on the island, also transforms into a spiritual leader for several of the young men: He helps Charlie find the strength to become clean, assists Walt in mastering his supernatural gift and – in a ritual reminiscent of Native American rites of initiation – guides Boone to a vision that forces him to deal with his problematic relationship to his step-sister. Thus, though Locke is not the leader of the group – which is clearly Jack – he is a man of authority both for the survivors and for the viewers. In the mystery plot of the show, he has the task of the detective. Like the viewer, he is in search of the reasons for the survivors' being stranded on the island (Askwith 169). He tries to find explanations for the strange phenomena they encounter there. In other words, he is the character the viewer expects to unravel "the truth." This truth is what he explains to Jack at the end of season one in a discussion where "not-so-deep issues like the importance of faith" (Hendershot no pag.) are pondered.

The episode dramatizes a significant conflict between Jack Shepherd and John Locke, which leads Locke to dub himself a "man of faith" and Jack "a man of science." This conflict between two central figures of the show can be read as a reference to a central contradictory, yet persistent feature in American national identity – the co-existence of religious faith and trust in scientific progress as the key cultural tenet of American national identity. Wilfred McClay explains that though the United States is committed to secularism, this "does not necessarily mean the separation of religion from public life" (para 8). On the contrary,

[i]n the United States religious belief has proven amazingly persistent even as the culture has been more and more willing to embrace enthusiastically all or most of the scientific and technological agenda of modernity. Sometimes the two reinforce one another. Sometimes they clash with one another, but the American culture has found room for both to be present. (ibid.)

With McClay's suggestion in mind, one can read the seemingly irreconcilable conflict between Jack Shepherd and John Locke as one which probably does not need a resolution in the series but can continue to exist whilst both retain their status as "leading men." Both of them are personifications of one particular cultural principle, science and faith respectively, which may often clash Yet, the series offers "room for both of them to be present," thus reaffirming that the co-existence of science and faith is possible within the discourse of American national identity.

Taking a closer look at how the conflict between Jack and Locke plays out, what becomes clear is that Locke does not stand for a particular faith, such as Catholicism, Protestantism or Hinduism, but can be read as a representation of a version of American civil religion. As Bellah explains, the term civil religion was introduced by Rosseau and refers to a collection of simple religious dogmas: "the existence of God, the life to come, the reward of virtue and the punishment of vice, and the exclusion of religious intolerance" (172). As already seen in the quote from Franklin's autobiography, American civil religion has also come to include the idea of providence, which is more often extended into the idea of the American people as chosen by God. These ideas have been evoked by American presidents from Washington to Lincoln to Kennedy (Bellah *passim*) up to Obama, who closed his Inaugural Address with a vision for the future in the spirit of civil religion and the ideals of his presidential predecessors:

America, in the face of our common dangers, in this winter of our hardship, let us remember these timeless words [of "the father of our nation"]; with hope and virtue, let us brave once more the icy currents, and endure what storms may come; let it be said by our children's children that when we were tested we refused to let this journey end, that we did not turn back nor did we falter; and with eyes fixed on the horizon and God's grace upon us, we carried forth that great gift of freedom and delivered it safely to future generations. (3)

Obama renders a situation of communal crisis, the "winter of our hardships," as a test that demands endurance and sacrifice to "carry forth" with "grace upon us," and the grace is granted by a higher power. The same approach fuels Locke's view in his faith-inspired debate on the meaning of their stay upon the island with the "man of science," Jack:

LOCKE: I think that's why you and I don't see eye to eye sometimes, Jack. Because you're a man of science.

JACK: Yeah. And what does that make you?

LOCKE: Me? Well, I'm a man of faith. Do you really think all this is an accident? That we, a group of strangers, survived, many of us with just superficial injuries? You think we crashed on this place by coincidence? Especially this place? We were brought here for a purpose, for a reason – all of us. Each one of us was brought here for a reason.

JACK: Brought here. And who brought us here, John?

LOCKE: The island. The island brought us here. This is no ordinary place. You've seen that. I know you have. The island chose you, too, Jack. It's destiny. ("Exodus" Part 3)

This dialogue resonates with foundational religious concepts that ground American national identity in a barely disguised form. What Locke proposes here is that the survivors are literally "elect people" who have landed on a place pre-destined for them. While he is clearly talking about some kind of mysterious providence, God is erased from the equation and replaced with "the island" (cf. "the island brought us here"). Yet, if one puts God back into this equation, the belief Locke expresses turns out to be founded on the principle that helped not just the "Founding Fathers" of the nation "to brave the icy current" but even earlier, the Puritan settlers to confront the "Wilderness" – a belief in Predestination, in the sense of their ordeals that were chosen not by them but for them, and an understanding of misfortunes and hardships as tests to prove themselves in the eyes of God and the world. The series' script positions the islanders in the place of Winthrop and his fellow Puritans who set out for America and had to

... consider that wee shall be as a citty upon a hill. The eies of all people are uppon us. Soe that if wee shall deale falsely with our God in this worke wee haue undertaken, and soe cause him to withdrawe his present help from us, wee shall be made a story and a by-word through the world. Wee shall open the mouthes of enemies to speake evill of the wayes of God, and all professors for God's sake. (Winthrop 304)

Although, strictly speaking, in the series the "eies of all [viewers] are upon" the islanders and judge their "deal[ings]" according to secular Western standards, the religious overtones in presenting the islanders as "chosen" people are hard to overlook. This also goes for Locke's mysterious statement, "We were brought here for a reason." This supplies a rationale for the "election" of the group which resonates with Cotton Mather's explanation of the frightening witchcraft incidents among the descendants of the first Puritan immigrants in Salem in 1692/3. In "The Wonders of the Invisible World" Mather explains witchcraft as an "attempt," that is a test to be suffered patiently in order to enjoy happiness and peace afterwards:

Wherefore the devil is now making one attempt more upon us; an attempt more difficult, more surprising, more snarled with unintelligible circumstances than any that we have hitherto encountered; an attempt so critical, that if we get well through, we shall soon enjoy halcyon days with all the vultures of hell trodden under our feet. (Mather 489)

The fact that the chosen people experience hardships and misery is in both cases taken not as a reason to doubt the covenant (with God or the island/destiny) but, paradoxically, as a reaffirmation that the American people must be the chosen ones. When Jack refers to a moment of crisis, a situation when his life was endangered by a mysterious "thing" on the island, he cannot shake Locke's belief in destiny. Locke immediately integrates this event into his belief system by re-interpreting it as a test by the island.

JACK: Look, I need for you to – I need for you to explain to me what the hell's going on inside your head, John. I need to know why you believe that that thing wasn't gonna-

LOCKE: (interrupts) I believe that I was tested. ("Exodus" Part 3)

What is more, when challenged, Locke defends his faith in destiny by introducing the notion of sacrifice as part of the predestined plan. Though Jack tries to give Locke another example to disprove the work of providence, or rather of "destiny" on the island by mentioning the sad death of Locke's mentee Boone on the island, Locke still will not digress from his convictions.

JACK: Did you talk with Boone about destiny, John?

LOCKE: Boone was a sacrifice that the island demanded. What happened to him at that plane was a part of a chain of events that led us here. That led us down a path. That led you and me to this day, to right now.

JACK: Where does that path end, John?

81

LOCKE: The path ends at the hatch. The hatch, Jack. All of it happened so that we could open the hatch.

JACK: No, no, we're opening the hatch so that we can survive.

LOCKE: Survival is all relative, Jack.

JACK: I don't believe in destiny.

LOCKE: Yes, you do. You just don't know it yet.

("Exodus" Part 3)

Sacrifice as understood here by Locke, is another key element of American civil religion. The loss of Boone is integrated by Locke into his firm belief in the island's, respectively destiny's plan for the islanders, just as Bellah shows Abraham Lincoln to integrate slavery and the terrors of the Civil War into his unshakable belief in God. In his speech in Independence Hall in Philadelphia on February 22, 1861, Lincoln interpreted both slavery and the war as part of God's "providence":

If we shall suppose that American slavery is one of those offenses which, in the providence of God, must needs come, but which, having continued through His appointed time, He now wills to remove, and that He gives to both North and South this terrible war as the woe due to those by whom the offense came, shall we discern therein any departure from those divine attributes which the believers in a living God always ascribe to Him? Fondly do we hope, fervently do we pray, that this mighty scourge of war may speedily pass away. Yet, if God wills that it continue until all the wealth piled by the bondsman's two hundred and fifty years of unrequited toil shall be sunk, and until every drop of blood drawn with the lash shall be paid by another draw with the sword, as was said three thousand years ago, so still it must be said "the judgements of the Lord are true and righteous altogether." (Lincoln qtd. in Bella 177)

Note that even the doubt in the workings of God's providence, which parallels Jack's doubt in "destiny" in the series, is present in Lincoln's reference to "departure from those divine attributes which the believers in a living God always ascribe to Him." But just like Locke in the series, Lincoln holds that whatever has to be sacrificed, it is the appropriate price ("woe") to be paid, even if he – unlike Locke – supports this claim with a reference to the bible.

Just as the original religious beliefs about the Puritans' mission in New England were thoroughly transformed to become part of the American civil religion, "a collection of beliefs, symbols, and rituals with respect to sacred things, [. . .] institutionalized in a collectivity" (Bellah 175) – John Locke's proto-religious assumptions are turned into a secularized discourse about the "lost" people's purpose on the island. While *Lost* thus appeals to basic features of an assumedly genuine American character and fate that can be traced back to key moments in the nation's history, *Lost* universalizes this experience and hides its historic origins and tradition.

Thus, the efforts to make meaning after having landed on a strange shore, remote from civilization and threatened from all sides, become an experience that easily translates to non-American viewers. Everybody with a TV can relate to the struggle for survival in the wilderness, conflicts with the "natives" of an island and the possibility of infection with yet unknown diseases. This has enabled the show to become an economic success on the international market, while it resonates reassuringly with familiar values and world-views with American audiences. While the show's mix of an ensemble cast appeals to viewers all over the world due to their different social, ethnic, national and religious backgrounds, the hegemonial centre of the community clearly is American. Newbury's thesis of the privileging of a "mythological, narrative of multicultural absorption into American nationhood" clearly also holds true for the treatment of religion in *Lost*, which is based upon the subtle representation of American civil religion, while it extrapolates and thereby to a certain extent "others" Catholicism.

Conclusion: The Function of Religion in *Lost*

Lost's grounding in civil religion, a discourse that has always grounded American political rhetoric in times of crisis, has severely contributed to its overwhelming appeal. It was conceived and first aired in the aftermath of 9/11. While this crisis produced many critical voices that interrogated America's changing position in a changing world, it also led to very conservative reactions. Notably George W. Bush's "Address to the Nation in Light of the Terrorist Attacks of September 11" immediately rendered the events in evangelical religious terms of "good" versus "evil," "us" versus "them" on the very day of the attacks. He translated the complex motivations for the act of international terrorism into terrorist hatred against the U.S.A. as "the brightest beacon for freedom and opportunity in the world" that "no one will keep [. . .] from shining" (para 2), and when he addressed "America and our friends and allies," he turned to the very Psalm that the producers of *Lost* chose to help Charlie and Eko calm their distress. Said the President: "And I pray they [the bereaved] will be comforted by a power greater than any of us, spoken through the ages in Psalm 23: 'Even though I walk through the valley of the shadow of death, I fear no evil, for You are with me'" (para. 6). This concurrence is more than just a coincidence but indicates a common strategy of conflict resolution in the President's and the series' recourse to religion in order to retrieve and reaffirm a shaken identity.

Lost's representational function as instruction for crisis management emerges right at the beginning of the story. Already within the first frames the viewers are presented with a setting that would have been edited out from any movie in the weeks directly after 9/11 – yet, here we are in 2004, with a depiction of a plane crash that revels in the chaos, panic and trauma caused by this catastrophe. For almost ten minutes the beginning sequence dwells on the burning plane wreck, screaming, desperate and injured survivors, all framed by the disquieting noise of the plane's turbine.

After the first shock of arrival has passed, John Locke already explains to Jack how to draw a meaning from this traumatic experience. Thereby John's belief is the key offered to the viewer to make sense out of inexplicable and tragic events.

LOCKE: This place is different, it's special. [...] we all know it, we all feel it. [...] What if everything that happened here, happened for a reason? ("White Rabbit")

As one online reviewer puts it, "the characters of 'Lost' are navigating a world where every minute detail – from their friends to their enemies to nature – is connected in a matrix of meaning for them. Everything is a clue. Everything has a place in context. There are no accidental encounters" (Bryant no pag.). To some extent the series is thus almost allegorical: The viewer is shown that there may be, or rather that there is meaning in a situation of crisis. Belief in providence/destiny develops in spite of the fact that this community has been hit by a catastrophe and is threatened from all sides. It incorporates this experience by reading it not as a reason to doubt destiny, but as a reaffirmation of its existence. *Lost*'s mass appeal with American audiences rests on its re-assurance of a world view where everything happens for a reason and every crisis, every catastrophe, is just a test.

Leigh Adams Wright, for instance, suggests that "[a] blatantly SF/fantasy show like *Lost* [...] never would have survived on a big-three network before the Twin Towers went down, much less become one of the most talked about [...] shows of the season" (87), but it did after 9/11 because viewers were then looking for meaning. While Wright concedes that "[a]ll narratives create meaning", she points out that "*Lost* is particularly explicit about doing so":

The relentless way in which even the most menial, inconsequential details of the survivors' lives seems to interconnect – from Sawyer's late night bar conversation with Jack's father to Hurley's lottery-winning appearance on a television screen in the house of the minister Jin was sent to kill – supercharges everything we see with importance, and lends the Lost characters' shared presence on the island an inevitability that speaks of something, some meaning, bigger than they are. (ibid.)

Hence, Locke's version of "truth," which is embedded in a specifically American civil religious rhetoric, gains authority over any other pattern of meaning production, because it coincides with the explicit narrative principle of the show itself. In other words, the way in which *Lost* is narrated works to reaffirm the notion of (divine) providence/destiny suggested by one of its characters. This belief is even more universally compatible when it is not only untied from any particular religious denomination but even from the notion of "God" himself, and remains simply bound to the very place the community lives in – "the island" that "chose us." The close relation of the show to a hegemonic American national identity and a dominant religion is blurred – it appears as a universal form of faith, a faith that is much wider and less dogmatic than, for instance, Catholicism, which is depicted as "other" and not "typically" American in the series.

As this analysis has shown, *Lost* offers a discourse of institutionalized religion through its Catholic characters Charlie and Eko and a discourse of civil religion as mouthed by John Locke and undergirding the narrative strategy of the show. Catholicism is marked excessively by the representational strategy. Its specific, extra-American historicity is stressed through the presentation of both its visual and oral tradition, and its cultural difference from other belief systems is shown through visualizing how deeply its followers are engrossed in its elaborate and spectacular system of signs. Furthermore, Catholicism is associated with "foreigners" (i.e. an Englishman and a Nigerian) and is thus rendered exotic.

The American John Locke, on the other hand, firmly believes in and promotes central Protestant ideas that are in accordance with basic American private and civil religious beliefs, such as *(divine)providence* and *the elect*. While the foreigners are explicitly presented as "religious," the American is not. Hence, his ideas are presented – in contrast to Charlie's and Eko's beliefs – as if they were not embedded in a specific religious context, as if they were "natural" and did not put a particular perspective on the world. As Locke's unmarked world view merges with and expresses the underlying meaning-making and assuring strategy of the post-9/11production, it becomes the unacknowledged key to the series' meaning. Thereby *Lost* reaffirms a hegemonic American national world view by obscuring its religious grounding and coding it as universal. The series' refashioning of a national crisis as personal moral trial and sense-seeking frontier experience appeals to a broad audience inside and outside of the U.S., while its negotiations of marked "other" versus unmarked "American" religious discourse hide its nationalist preoccupations from a questioning gaze. Read like this, *Lost* can be understood as a conservative reaction to the crisis of 9/11 that helps code a secular national catastrophe in terms of a quasi-religious test for the chosen American people.

Works Cited

Adams Wright, Leigh. "There Are No Coincidences. Making Meaning in *Lost*." *Getting Lost. Survival, Baggage and Starting Over in J.J. Abram's Lost*. Ed. Orson Scott Card. Dallas: Benbella Books, 2006. 85-90. Print.

Askwith, Ian. "'Do You Even Know Where This Is Going?' *Lost's* Viewers and Narrative Pre-mediation." *Reading Lost Perspectives on a Hit Television Show.* Ed. Robert Pearson. London: Tauris, 2009. 159-180. Print.

Bellah, Robert N. *Beyond Belief. Essays on Religion in a Post-Traditional World.* New York: Harper and Row, 1920. 168-186. Print.

Bryant, Stephen. "Why ABC's 'Lost' is the Future of Online Media." *Publish.* 4 May 2006. Web. 18 Sept. 2007.

Bush, George W. "9/11 Address to the Nation. 'A Great People Has Been Moved to Defend a Great Nation.' 11 September 2001. *American Rhetoric. Online Speech Bank.* 2001. Web. 4 Aug. 2011.

Hendershot, Heather. "Gender and Genre in *Lost* and *Battlestar Gallactica.*" *Flow TV.* University of Texas. 2006. Web. 18 Sept. 2007.

Keveney, Bill. "TV Hits Maximum Occupancy." *USA Today.* 11 Aug. 2005. Web. 9 Jul. 2007.

Mather, Cotton. "The Wonders of the Invisible World." *The Heath Anthology of American Literature.* Vol. 1. 4th ed. Eds. Paul Lauter et al. Boston: Houghton Mifflin, 2002. 497-504. Print.

McClay, Wilfred: "Religion and Secularism. The American Experience." *Pew Forum Faith Angle Conference, Key West, Florida, 3 December 2007.* 8 Jan. 2008. Web. 11 Jul. 2011.

Newbury, Michael: *"Lost* in the Orient: Transnationalism Interrupted." *Reading Lost Perspectives on a Hit Television Show.* Ed. Robert Pearson. London: Tauris, 2009. 201-221. Print.

Obama, Barack. "Transcript: Barack Obama's Inaugural Address," *New York Times.* 20 Jan. 2009, Web. 26 Aug. 2010.

"Pilot Part 1," "White Rabbit," "The Moth," "Exodus Part 3". *Lost.* Season 1. Buena Vista Home Entertainment, 2005. DVD.

"The 23rd Psalm," "Fire and Water." *Lost.* Season 2 (part one). Buena Vista Home Entertainment, 2005. DVD.

Winthrop, John: "A Modell of Christian Charity." *The Heath Anthology of American Literature.* Vol. 1. 4th ed. Eds. Paul Lauter et al. Boston: Houghton Mifflin, 2002. 296-304. Print.

Religion and the Body

The Link between Eating Disorders and Religion: Re-encoding the Urge for Thinness

PETRA DANIELCZYK

When it comes to food and the body, Christians have to address manifold questions. The fundamentalist nutritionist Gwen Shamblin with her "Weigh Down" program knows all the right answers: All food is given by God, which also means that none of it is "not good for us." The body is likewise a gift of God. It is given to us not for personal use but as His temple to be filled by Him. Eating disorders like anorexia and bulimia are thus not illnesses but signs of straying from the Lord's path and they can be overcome by turning back to Him. All this is carefully spelled out in Shamblin's self-help book *The Weigh Down Diet* and propagated by the so called Remnant fellowship, a movement she has founded.

But why do Christian fundamentalists turn to dieting, and in its course, to eating disorders? What is the link between food consumption and religion? Why can Shamblin's advice sometimes lead to overcoming the illnesses? Are there links between the treatment and basic mechanisms of fundamentalist dogma? And how does this tie in with contemporary American culture? This paper will pursue these questions by juxtaposing Shamblin's and secular, feminist and cultural studies explanations of eating disorders. It will investigate her program and its roots in popular culture and Puritan ideals. Finally, it will take a critical look at the reasons that enable self-declared prophets like Shamblin to step into society's spotlight.

I will begin with a short characterization of eating disorders and a description of their medical treatment. The factors that link religious thought to eating disorders are outlined in the second part of the paper. It starts by explaining Gwen Shamblin's faith-based "Weigh Down Diet," discusses the major aspects of the method and finally presents two testimonies by Remnant fellowship members who successfully fought their eating disorders and a negative assessment by a former follower who left the fellowship. In the conclusion I will answer the question why and how U.S. religious belief has to be taken into account when dealing with eating disorders in U.S. culture.

The focus on women throughout my paper is not to suggest that men are not affected. It is due to the fact that many more women than men are suffering from eating disorders, that medical research and cultural studies have concentrated on them, as well as on diet programs that mainly target women.

The Disease

Nearly five percent of young U.S. women and adolescents suffer from anorexia and up to 20 percent of college women suffer from bulimia (Lelwica 180). According to the "anred.com" website by the National Association for Anorexia Nervosa and Associated Eating Disorders Inc., which is a non-profit organization that provides information about anorexia nervosa, bulimia nervosa, binge eating disorder and compulsive exercising, about 50% of the people who have been anorexic develop bulimia or bulimic patterns (ibid). Eating disorders occur at a frequency far greater than usually realized and are difficult to cure. The most common forms are anorexia and bulimia nervosa.

Anorexia nervosa is characterized by weight loss, body image disturbance and a morbid fear of weight gain. As a result, puberty is delayed, hormones are disturbed and sex drives either disappear or diminish. The person suffering from anorexia will deny the dangers of low weight because she/he is terrified of gaining weight. He or she will report feeling fat even if emaciated (ibid). Symptoms of the disease include depression, irritability, withdrawal and peculiar behaviors such as compulsive rituals, strange eating habits and division of foods into 'good/safe' and 'bad/dangerous' categories (ibid).

Bulimia nervosa is characterized by binge eating and compensatory purging by vomiting, use of laxatives, diuretics, or diet pills, exercise or fasting. While eating, the person usually feels out of control (ibid). Individuals concerned have problems with impulse control. "anred.com" states that though theses individuals seem happy on the outside they lead a double life: They are insecure on the inside and often haunted by anxiety, depression, self-doubt and deeply buried anger.

Eating disorders are diseases which almost always begin in adolescence and continue throughout adulthood (Gerlinghoff 20). Often they are combined with other psychiatric illnesses like obsessive-compulsive disorders, depression or substance abuse (22). In general, eating disorders are persistent diseases with an aptness to relapses and chronic characteristics (23).

Eating disorders are clearly linked to cultural body ideals. Today thinness, in particular women's thinness has risen to superior status in Western cultures. Feminist critics have pointed out the connections between eating disorders, strategies of social control and the subjugation of women. In her book *Unbearable Weight*, Susan Bordo argues that the cult of thinness is actually symbolic of the fear of women's fat and a means to contain women's power. Thus, as women gain power in society, their bodies are meant to dwindle and suffer. She states that

female hunger – for public power, for independence, for sexual gratification – [must] be contained, and the public space that women be allowed to take up be circumscribed, limited [...]. On the body of the anorexic woman such rules are grimly and deeply etched. (171)

Naomi Wolf has a similar explanation of the social origins of eating disorders. In *The Beauty Myth* she states: "a cultural fixation on female thinness is not an obsession about female beauty but an obsession about female obedience" (187). Women who remain thin are being obedient; it is another way for patriarchy to control them. "If women cannot eat the same food as men, we cannot experience equal status in the community" (189).

The reasons for developing eating disorders can be neither reduced solely to social nor to biological roots. Scientists sketch a multidimensional model of origin, including biological, psychosocial and socio-cultural factors (Gerlinghoff, Backmund 25). They point out two common denominators of people suffering from eating disorders: They have an urge for perfectionism and they feel worthless (Claude-Pierre 53). In other words – no matter what the causes and triggers of the disease are – dissatisfaction with and insecurity about one's status in the family, at school or work and in society at large lead to a lack of feeling self-worth and a general lack of control. This unsatisfactory state is compensated by taking charge over a part of one's life that is at first glance, relatively easy to control – the body, which becomes a substitute battle ground for the status fights not fought with others. Hence the anorectic or bulimic person leads a 'double life': While actually hurting the body, the disease becomes a secret friend. Hidden from family and friends, it gives an inner strength that helps to compensate negative feelings and develop more confidence. But "Mr. Jekyll" soon turns into "Mr. Hyde." What once was controllable soon controls the individual: The whole life centers around food and the rituals connected to it.

People with eating disorders believe they are capable of ending their double life from one day to the next, but this is erroneous (Gerlinghoff, Backmund 27). Without the compulsion, they feel empty and alone, while the compulsivity of 'having to do it' keeps them in the grip of the disease (ibid). Eating disorders are highly psychosomatic, that is "illnesses having both physical and mental components [...] involving a physical condition caused or aggravated by mental or emotional disorder" (Brown 2402). The disturbed interaction between the ill person, her/his body and social environment cannot be treated by just taking pills. Psychotherapy is therefore an integral part of curing the disturbed psychic balance (Gerlinghoff, Backmund 40).

Yet where do these insights leave us with regard to the connection between religion, thinness, and the cure of eating disorders? The link seems to be twofold: Firstly, with regard to the general function of spiritual belief systems, religion has not only served to stabilize and legitimize institutions and values of the whole of society but also to found the social identity of each of its members (Peters 230). In a food-related crisis of identity, religion and its institutions may aid in regaining one's psychic balance. More specifically in the history of Christianity, exercising control over one's body and its needs has been regulated by various rules and rituals, which include instructions about dealing with "clean and unclean" food. Hence, the psycho-social function of religion and the traditions of dietaries supply the link to individual food regulations and their effects.

Secondly, with regard to food as a cultural value and meaning system in itself: for an ill person, the strict regulation of food intake and its effect on her/his body may become a way to organize the world and help to cope with it, a means to salvation. The pursuit of thinness displays many characteristics of a religious self-optimizing technique, even though few followers of the slimness cult would identify themselves as followers of a religion.

I will now explore how these basic connections play out in the fundamentalist approach of Gwen Shamblin's *Weigh Down Diet*. Christian fundamentalism is in this paper understood as the belief that claims to be is based entirely on the fundamentals and traditions of the Bible, promotes the literal understanding of it and opposes modernization and secularization (cf. Peters 79-80).

Eating Disorders and Fundamentalism
"you do not have a disease"

Eating disorders are as much a problem of Christians as of other people, especially teens. Yet Christian fundamentalists tend to explain them "as problems that are induced by the secular world that can be cured by religion" (Hendershot 99). They criticize society's pressure on women to have a certain kind of body as secular superficiality. As a remedy, the study of the Bible is meant to show girls that their bodies are "temples of the Holy Spirit" (ibid). Cultural critic Heather Hendershot explains that fundamentalists neither connect the reasons for eating disorders to religion (ibid), nor to fundamentalist "family pressure, an authoritarian home-life, or the tremendous pressures that being a 'good Christian' can entail" (ibid). She asks:

Might resistance to giving all control to God be a contributing factor to developing eating disorders in the first place? Or might the imperative to surrender oneself spiritually actually contribute to a woman's desire to have total control over her earthly body? (ibid)

It is striking that Shamblin starts from exactly these links between taking control and eating disorders in her book *The Weigh Down Diet*, yet she draws radically different conclusions.

Shamblin's Christian faith-based weight loss program has been in existence since 1986 (http://weighdown.com/About_Us.shtml, 02.08.08). She promotes it in the media (e.g.: NBC's Today Show, The Tyra Banks Show), there are local and online classes as well as "at home kits" (http://weighdown.com/Find_A_Class.shtml, 02.08.08). The "pioneers of faith-based weight loss" sell the "Weigh Down and Strongholds at Home Package Special" for only $109.99 (ibid) and Shamblin's books range from $13.00 up to $19.99. Helping people losing weight appears to be good business.

In his critical study *Our Own Private Exodus*, Gregor Schrettle points out that Shamblin is in fact not the first "pioneer" of Bible-based religious dieting, because "the roots of this genre date back to the middle of the twentieth century"(Schrettle 17). He underlines especially the "somewhat paradoxical double status" (23) of *The Weigh Down Diet*, which fuses U.S. consumer culture and a critique of it (ibid) and works both as a religious cure *in* and *of* popular culture. The program buys into and profits from the Puritan legacy and a modified version of its ideal of asceticism that is still prevalent in American popular culture (150-151): Fulfillment through consumption goes hand in hand with a feeling of normally subconscious reprehensibility if consumption is not practiced out of need but solely for pleasure's sake (ibid). Thus obesity is understood as a sign of sinfulness that hints at undisciplined overeating for pleasure, "The attack on fat" is the logical conclusion (152). By participating in the diet craze, Shamblin's "Weigh Down Diet" is "a case of religion *in* popular culture" (96-97, emphasis added) and it actualizes pop culture's dormant Puritan roots. The secular dieter diets for her/himself in the name of thinness, but the Christian dieter goes one step further and seeks, by purging her/his lust just like the Puritan forefathers did, for a superior godliness.

Yet Shamblin, at the same time, criticizes eating disorders as a result of the popular diet and health food craze. Thereby she comes close to cultural critics like Bordo, who have shown that anorexia and bulimia result from the world of consumption; anorexia denies the self and represses the desire to consume food, bulimia is the unstable double bind between the embrace of consumer capitalism and its refusal (binging and purging of consumption) (Bordo 201). Shamblin reacts by offering a religious cure *of* popular culture. She presents eating disorders as curable aberrations from the natural and right, i.e. God's way to live and eat. She denies the psychosomatic reality of the illnesses:

Once you have been labeled as bulimic, anorexic, or obese, and then read current theories that you are genetically overweight, you could really feel trapped. Who could muster up the energy to combat chronic genetic obesity, bulimia, or anorexia nervosa that is genetic or inherited? (Shamblin 37)

She claims, "I have seen people diagnosed with anorexia and bulimia who have not had more episodes" after they enrolled in her program (38-39). Obviously Shamblin does not identify eating disorders as illnesses, especially not as physiological ones. She denies medical diagnoses and questions the scientific explanations mainly because they do not include God. She accuses the "labeling" by the secular culture as "devitalizers." In contrast, she advertises her religious program as a revitalizing cure to problems that secular culture cannot heal. Step for step she translates medical classifications into a terminology of sin, guilt, and repentance – key Puritan concepts. Eating disorders become "bingeing" and "purging" and "First of all," the bulimic, anorexic or overweight person has to "understand that [they] do not have a disease" (102).

So what is the root of the problem? It is what your *heart* is depending on! Bingeing is [...] a *spiritual dependency* on these foods for comfort and love. [...] And purging not some disease or obsession. It is all a consequence of your *lust* for food. (103, emphasis added)

The cure of what is not a physiological problem anymore is then purely spiritual:

1. You can *repent* (turn back to God), ask for His help, and simply wait until your body empties again. [...] do not worry – you will be fine. *You must practice being dependent on God.* If you call out to God, He can give you the peace you need and the *control feeling* you are looking for – with no *guilt*. In other words, God can make you feel better than purging.
2. Or you can *bypass God* [...] and take the purging route. This second option is obviously never-ending because it does not address or uproot the *lust* for food. (103-104, emphasis added)

By using trigger words such as "lust" and "sin" she marks the eating disorders as blasphemous actions against God. To stop "bingeing" and "purging" and regain a "control feeling" is thus redefined as personal salvation from the sins of gluttonous self-indulgence, carnal rebellion and hypocrisy. The only salvation, and at the same time the only effective cure is said to be repentance and "practice being dependent on God." This solution is choice number 1. It is juxtaposed against solution number 2, which by "bypass[ing] God" is no solution/cure at all.

Shamblin writes for a wide audience. She addresses the widespread longing to lose weight in Christian and non-Christian U.S. citizens. At the same time she grasps hold of her Christian audience by appealing to their eternal souls. Only God can give "the control feeling" one is "looking for" according to her. And she promises a miraculous healing:

After years of purging, some people seem to automatically throw up after a meal. This is reverse peristalsis. Just don't worry about it – your body is confused now, but it will settle back down to normal forward-moving peristalsis. (104)

This claim is against all medical evidence and therefore dangerously misleading. Yet the religious promise is rhetorically substantiated by a mix of expert and lay language. A term like "peristalsis," which denotes the intestinal movement, is meant to impress her readers. It underlines that she, as a registered nutritionist, must know more about what is good for the human body. At the same time she uses colloquial phrases like "Just don't worry" and simplifying metaphors like "your body is confused" by which she gains the empathy of her numerous readers. This is her definition of eating disorders in the book:

Obsessive behavior includes excessive exercise, starvation diets, or consumption of laxatives [...] Bulimia, or purging, is what I call a second-generation disorder. You saw your mother or father overeat and then try to solve the problem with a diet sheet. They only got bigger, so you (the next generation) got smart and said, "Diets are not really working, so I will throw up (purge) or take a laxative." (104-105)

[...] anorexia nervosa is a condition wherein the person refuses to eat as the body calls for food so that the person becomes extraordinarily thin. This behavior is successful in drawing attention; however, the anorexic person needs to know that this behavior will not be rewarded by God with the acceptance that is needed. (224)

In both quotes, Shamblin establishes her nutritionist authority by characterizing certain symptoms of bulimia and anorexia, only to then play down their seriousness by reducing them to a coping strategy with parental behavior and an effort to draw attention. While parental examples are certainly influential, more than experiencing one's parents' diets is at stake in bulimia. And while the effort to draw attention can be one reason behind anorexia, it is not the only one. These are laymen's myths which can lead to lethal outcomes.

Shamblin's inclusion of exercise in the anorectic behavior is explained by Schrettle as another revival of Puritan thought, for exercising, unless for rational purposes, was considered idle pleasures (132-133). The body is seen as pulling the mind away from God and thus needs to be reduced to a functional device. The physical (the urge to move as much as to eat) needs to be replaced by the spiritual. Hence, Shamblin advises "Replace the intensive desire to eat with an intensive desire for God, and the bingeing will end. As a result, the bulimia will subside" (105). Readers might, in fact, be stunned by the simplicity of her suggestions:

We are emphatically telling you that you can eat whatever your body is calling for and that you do not have to make the food righteous ever again. Do not be afraid of the fats and sugars. You are not addicted to them; you just want them excessively because you have not been allowed to have them for so long. (105)

The sudden assuring change to "We" compared to the "I" that is used in the more scientifically inclined passages, should caution the readers. Who is speaking here? – Shamblin the scientific nutritionist, Shamblin the prophet of her Church or the salesperson Gwen and "her program." While people that have suffered from weight problems are meant to be assured in this paragraph that they (or rather "we") have found a solution to their problem that includes even the eating of fats and sugars, it should give them pause that Shamblin at the moment of imparting *her* solution/cure changes her rhetorical register to using the Royal '*we*' with special emphasis added – "we are *emphatically* telling you." The (far too) simple message seems to need an extra rhetorical push.

"What do You want, God? Your will not mine"

While eating (or not) is made to seem almost unproblematic, "you can eat whatever your body is calling for," the real problem for Shamblin (and the Christian fundamentalist) is "sin":

The law of *sin* (overeating, smoking, alcohol overindulgence, drug overindulgence, materialism etc.) is [...] real, it is strong, it pulls you down, and it is a force that must be reckoned with. [...], you can ignore the law of sin (the magnetic pull to the worldly things) and come to an early spiritual *death*. (129, emphasis added)

The way to salvation lies in "mental exercise" (131) and breaking "away from the pull of the world [...] to focus on what your heavenly Father wants. Keep[ing the] mind centered every day by asking Him, "What do You want, God? Your will not mine." (131)

As Schrettle argues, for Shamblin obedience and submissiveness are the central human qualities (41). She claims that to convert "our" love for the refrigerator, "we need to obey God" (Shamblin 149). Obedience will lead to loving him more and more each time, as to be read in the Bible, Hebrews 11:6: "He rewards those who earnestly seek Him." She states: "We fall in love through obedience, or keeping commands" (149) and points out that obedience measures the love for God in your heart (150). The obedient and unselfish will reach paradise on earth, even if this might not always by easy: "Christ's followers must be willing to embrace pain – there is no backing out" (177). Mankind is just "bucking stallions that need to submit to the rider's hand" (ibid) and "Self-denial is also a part of the will of the Father. If we made Him happy, then we will be at peace with ourselves" (187).

Yet Shamblin's credo of self-denial is not gender-neutral. By quoting 1 Peter 3:1-6, she orders "Wives, in the same way [to] be submissive to [their] husbands." What has the female subjugation to a husband to do with the liberation from "the lust" for food? As Schrettle argues, women have long been interpreted as being closer to the body than men. Their greater proneness to sin was always thought to be in need of immediate male control (174).

Yet the ultimate "master" remains God, as Shamblin argues with reference to the Biblical theme of serving two masters, one of which you cannot love without hating the other. "What wonderful news," she announces,

as you love God, you will not be able to bow down to the brownies! It will be repulsive to eat the second half of the hamburger. You will despise worshiping the food. You cannot serve both God and someone or something else, therefore, the Promised Land is in sight – you will lose weight! (http://www.beliefnet.com/story/8/story_836_1.html).

Here the central contradiction in Shamblin's approach is put into a nutshell: while the earthly delights – brownies, hamburger, and food in general – are rejected, the announcement of the Promised Land is equated with earthly (versus spiritual) and outward (versus "inner") success – weight loss. Shamblin bluntly connects morality, the soul and paradise with thinness. She has a spiritual program with a material aim. This is not only a weird connection for a fundamentalist Christian but a potential reinforcement of the urge of anorectics and bulimics to control their life and status via weight reduction. If weight reduction for non-Christian persons suffering from eating disorders appears as a way to personal self-improvement and control, according to Shamblin it is the reward for religious self-improvement and the surrendering of control to God. She re-encodes the urge for thinness from secular to religious plane, but thereby does not necessarily diminish the urge.

This makes one wonder if the program is really appropriate for people suffering from eating disorders. It is difficult to read the simplifying, highly emphatic, and contradictory messages about right and wrong ways to cure eating disorders without a feeling of anxiety, especially if one keeps in mind that they are directed at seriously ill people. And if eating disorders are to be cured "simply" by believing in God and letting go of one's secular self (to be later awarded with "weight loss"), this might strengthen the problems that lead to eating disorders in the first place – namely the lack of a meaningful structure, a focus to get through the day and the feeling of self-worth and appraisal by society.

The Remnant fellowship, a group founded by Shamblin, has its own website with testimonies of success. Two of these will now be introduced and discussed.

Example 1: Cindy Ellis, healed from bulimia and addictions (emphasis added)

[…] Before I knew the truth about God's sweet laws, there was much evil and much pain in my heart. *My sins enslaved me. And there were many […] a constant focus on myself before God, greed for food, bulimia, overdrinking, sexual sins, lust, laziness, gossip and slander, unforgiveness, lying, grumbling, complaining, and a generally ungrateful heart.* It is disgusting to think that these things accompanied me into any sanctuary in which I claimed to be worshiping and serving the Lord God Almighty and claimed loyalty to his son Jesus Christ who was perfect in obedience to our amazing Father. *No one could help me change or get away from my sin because none of them had lain down there [sic] own sins. We had all been taught that "we are only human" and "God knows you can't obey."* […]

Example 2: Suzanne Gentry, healed from depression, anxiety, bulimia (bold emphasis added)

From the age of 17, I was obsessed with thinness and learned ways to keep my weight down without having to starve myself. *I had so much greed for food that I knew I couldn't be a "successful anorexic", so bulimia was the eating disorder of choice for me. Over a few years I went from binging and vomiting, to taking massive amounts of laxatives (I even overdosed on them after taking 90 laxatives and almost died), to taking speed so that I wouldn't be hungry (and everything in between, including diet pills, diuretics, alcohol to numb out so I wouldn't feel hungry* [...]), [...] I knew from the start that all of this was wrong, so I pursued many different kinds of "therapy" and nothing worked. I was able to stop vomiting for periods of time, but I was *still obsessed with food and with staying thin*. [...] Then I found Weigh Down and realized that *until I changed my HEART, I would never be free from this life-stealing eating disorder. Weigh Down has not only given me freedom from bulimia, but has replaced it w/ a love for God* that I never had nor thought was even possible [...] I used [to] think God was supposed to zap me w/ His magic wand and make me "well" (*I believed this SIN was a "DISEASE"*), so when He didn't, I was just angry at Him and basically felt hopeless and lost. Now I know that I must commit my mind, heart, soul and strength to Him every single day, and THEN He will show me the truth, and the truth will (AND DOES) set me free!!![...] He has blessed me in unbelievable ways (i.e., I have a wonderful new home, a great job [...] and a husband who treats me so well and with whom I can share my love for God). (http://www.remnantfellowship.org/RFBA_Eating.asp)

In these testimonies we find an overabundance of cues how Christian fundamentalists like Shamblin view and mean to cure eating disorders. It is also obvious how they influence their followers.

Suzanne Gentry (example 2) states that she once wrongly believed the "SIN" was a disease she suffered from, thus she stopped "labeling" and "devitalizing" herself (Shamblin 38). She tells emphatically that "life goes SO much better if I seek His will, not my own" and that God has rewarded her hugely. Like Shamblin promised, the former bulimic "[r]eplace[d] the intensive desire to eat with an intensive desire for God, and the bingeing [...] end[ed]. As a result, the bulimia [...] subside[d]" (Shamblin 105, cf. above).

Gentry also reveals that the secular world made her "from the age of 17 [...] obsessed with thinness" and only when she found God and the Remnant fellowship was she "blessed" with the structure and appraisal (in the form of her husband, her job, a wonderful new home) she searched for. That she took drugs and used alcohol points to her secret double life as anorectic: While socially being acceptable and part of events she allowed her eating disorder to rule her. After her turn to God she found the love she could not find in society.

Cindy Ellis (example 1) states that "there was much evil and much pain in my heart," indicating that the "evil" and "pain" were obviously her fault. This, like Gentry's self-accusations, exemplifies that failure is attributed to the individual while success is attributed to God. This is an explanatory mechanism that is derived from the Puritan idea of individual responsibility, which has been transferred to American popular culture and is re-encoded by Shamblin for her dieting program (Schrettle 125). Ellis confesses that she sinned by constantly focusing on herself and a host of other "sins" followed suit: "greed for food, bulimia, overdrinking, etc." The list of Cindy's sins reads like an illustration of Shamblin's already quoted warning that

The law of *sin* (overeating, smoking, alcohol overindulgence, drug overindulgence, materialism etc.) is [...] real, it is strong, it pulls you down, and it is a force that must be reckoned with. (129, emphasis added)

It could be shown in further detail that the 'confessions' work just like footnotes that exemplify and propagate Shamblin's book.

Yet Ellis's advertisement for Shamblin's program goes one step further. She claims that even in the church ("any sanctuary") where she went for help before finding "The Weigh Down Diet," she did not find a solution for her problems but was told that "God knows you can't obey" (example 1). Thereby the helpful Christian perspective is narrowed down to Remnant's approach only, which makes the Remnant fellowship the only true, or at least the only useful church for people with problems like the ones characterized above.

This connects to another aim of Shamblin: making a profit from the Weigh Down program. Narrowing down the solution to weight problems solely to her church is the perfect business plan. Her followers will spend money only on her diet plan. Making a profit is not a problem in the eyes of Christian fundamentalists. As Schrettle points out in his study, religion and business have interacted and blended in manifold ways since the Puritans settled the Atlantic shores (140). Acquiring goods and wealth was then the outward sign for being elected by God and, in parallel fashion, a slim appearance marks spiritual success for Shamblin and her followers.

In order to find a negative example for the way Shamblin's diet works one has to look on other websites. The makers of SpiritWatch.org "formally called the Tennessee Valley Bible Students Association (TVBSA)" aim at "Countering the influence and spread of spiritually deceptive and religiously abusive groups that exist in the Tennessee Valley" and criticize the Weigh Down program and the Remnant fellowship. On SpiritWatch a former follower of the "Weigh Down Diet" reports her experiences:

So when I came back and continued conducting WD classes [...] I began to feel guilty about even thinking about food when I wasn't hungry, as a result I began dropping more weight. "One bite past full" or to "lust after" a meal that had not yet been given to me was disobedience. Sometimes, in the middle of a meal I wasn't sure if I was full or not and I'd take a bite and then realized "wait a minute, I was full!" and then it's too late, I took that bite! I had disobeyed. So I cut my food in half again, and then I started cutting my half in half and by that time I was cutting my fourth in half ... the portions were getting smaller and smaller because the guilt was getting more and more. ... while I may have been feeling guilty, people started seeing me dropping weight and would say, "oh wow, what's going on?" and then a new zeal would start. (http://spiritwatch.org/remnantcultism.htm)

In contrast to example 1 (Ellis), the focus on food had not waned but even gained importance in the life of the former follower, it had been worsened by the feeling of guilt. In this quote there is no praise for God but the horror of a life that is filled with the fear of disobedience. Instead of living balanced and eating normally the former member reports a food intake controlled by rules, not made by herself or God but by Gwen Shamblin in His name. Like all patients suffering from eating disorders she tells of a secret double life: On the outside she was dropping weight and people were amazed, but on the inside she felt traumatized by guilt. The guilt controlled her life. The emotional stress inflicted by the diet is shown to result in (a re-enforcement of) an eating disorder. Instead of presenting a cure, Shamblin's re-encoding of thinness as leading to Jesus is shown to lead (further in) to a psychosomatic disease.

Conclusion

Nowadays the wish for a thinner body is so overwhelming that in a religious country like the USA, 'prophets' such as Shamblin can have enormous success. Modified religious ideas (especially Puritan and Protestant concepts) underlie modern American popular culture. While religion normally tends to stabilize American society it can challenge American culture from within if it criticizes the mainstream (ibid 198). As this is what Shamblin's approach starts from, it has even a certain counter cultural quality, since secular American culture is criticized as lacking spiritual fulfillment (195).

Thus, I agree with Schrettle that religious dieting may be regarded as a culturally logical reaction to the economic abundance of the American twentieth and twenty-first centuries (157). Yet, fundamentalist approaches to the problem like Shamblin's "Weigh Down Diet" tend to posit one standard, inflexible and authoritarian moral code to cure highly individual, complex, psychosomatic illnesses that are caused and influenced by multiple social conditions. All in all, Shamblin's program rests on re-encoding the secular urge for thinness into a spiritual obsession. Her followers do not learn to confront the reasons and conditions that trigger the disease but are even additionally threatened by spiritual punishment and feelings of guilt should they sway from the newly gained spirituality. By "die[ing] to our will and get[ting] off the throne," having "[Him] put[ting] His great personality (Holy Spirit) in its place" (Shamblin 182), the lack of feeling self-worth and the general lack of control that are the sources of eating disorders are strongly re-enforced. Thus, even if Shamblin's program can help cure eating disorders, the success is dearly bought and might always lead to relapse.

Moreover, as Hendershot (99) indicates, teenagers from fundamentalist, heavily authoritarian homes are highly at risk to develop eating disorders as a form of rebellion that is rechanneled to be destructive for them and leave the (repressive) Christian surface order intact. 'Good' children, who strive for Christian perfection and would not want to reel openly against an order that they have learned is good and true, might be even more at risk than those with more relaxed attitudes.

For people suffering from eating disorders, a reorientation from their body to more spiritual interests may help. But a concentration on God alone will seldom be enough, and a shallow re-coding of thinness from worldly to religious concern runs the risk of leading to other addictions or mental illnesses. In so far as dieting may be considered as just another degree of an eating disorder since the body is under surveillance all the time, as Schrettle argues (182), the danger in religious dieting lies in a potential reinforcement of the urge of self-control and guilt about the loss of it. If weight reduction was formerly thought the way to personal self-improvement and -control, weight loss according to Shamblin becomes the reward for and the expression of the (re)turn to Christ. The anorectic's or bulimic's problems with food and the body are again emphasized, the close surveillance of the body is continued and the vicious circle of centering on food is reinforced.

Works Cited

Anorexia Nervosa and Related Eating Disorders, Inc. 2005. Web. 10 Aug. 2008.

Beliefnet. Inspiration. Spirituality. Faith. Beliefnet, Inc. Web. 10 Aug. 2008.

Bordo, Susan. *Unbearable Weight: Feminism, Western Culture, and the Body.* Berkeley: U of California P, 1993. Print.

Brown, Lesley. *The New Shorter Oxford English Dictionary on Historical Principles.* Oxford: Oxford UP, 1993. Print.

Claude-Pierre, Peggy, and Gabriele Herbst. *Der Weg zurück ins Leben. Magersucht und Bulimie verstehen und heilen.* Frankfurt a. M.: Fischer, 1998. Print.

Gerlinghoff, Monika, and Herbert Backmund. *Ess-Störungen. Fachwissen, Krankheitserleben, Ess-Programme.* Weinheim and Basel: Beltz, 2006. Print.

Hendershot, Heather. "Virgins for Jesus: the Gender Politics of Therapeutic Christian Fundamentalist Media." *Hop on Pop: The Politics and Pleasures of Popular Culture.* Eds. Henry Jenkins et al. Durham: Duke UP, 2002. 88-104. Print.

Lelwica, Michele M. "Losing their Way to Salvation. Women, Weight Loss, and the Salvation Myth of Culture Life." *Religion and Popular Culture in America.* Eds. Bruce David Forbes and Jeffrey H. Mahan. Berkeley and Los Angeles: U of California P, 2000. 180-200. Print.

Peters, U. *Grosses Wörterbuch Religion. Grundwissen von A-Z.* München: Compact, 2008. Print.

Shamblin, Gwen. *The Weigh Down Diet – Inspirational Way to Lose Weight, Stay Slim and Find a New You.* New York: Doubleday, 1997. Print.

Schrettle, G. *Our Own Private Exodus: Gwen Shamblin's Dieting Religion and America's Puritan Legacy.* Essen: Die Blaue Eule, 2006. Print.

Remnant Fellowship. Weigh Down Ministries. 2003-2007. Web. 10 Aug. 2008.

SpiritWatch Ministries. Web. 10 Aug. 2008.

Weigh Down Ministries. Weigh Down Ministries. Web. 2 Aug. 2008.

Wolf, Naomi. *The Beauty Myth: How Images of Beauty Are Used Against Women.* London: William Morrow, 1991. Print.

Identity, Morals, and Visibility: The Virginity Pledge Movement and Popular Culture

ELISA EDWARDS

"Believing that true love waits, I make a commitment to God, myself, my family, my friends, my future mate, and my future children to be sexually abstinent from this date until the day I enter a biblical marriage relationship." These were the words that were printed on 200,000 chastity pledge cards in July 1994. They were distributed to teenagers in a "True Love Waits" campaign which found its peak in a "weekend-long chastity extravaganza, featuring various speakers and the hottest Christian bands" (Hendershot, "Virgins for Jesus" 90).

This example demonstrates the increasing interaction between religion and popular culture in the U.S.A. As popular culture is marked by commercialism, entertainment, a "mass audience," and "technologies of mass distribution" (Forbes 3), it is often considered to be the opposite of high, i.e. respectable and valuable culture (Forbes 2). Religion, in contrast, can be understood as "an integrated system of belief, lifestyle, ritual activities, and institutions by which individuals give meaning to (or find meaning in) their lives by orienting themselves to what they take to be holy, sacred, or of the highest value" (Corbett 7). Yet, as Bruce David Forbes points out, there are at least four possible ways in which popular culture and religion can relate to one another: religion can be found in popular culture, popular culture can be part of religion, popular culture can be worshiped as a person's religion, and religion and popular culture can be in dialogue (10). In this paper, I will focus on popular culture in religion.

In a time in which all aspects of society have turned into "spectacle" (Debord 2), religion consequently is forced to participate in and make use of the contemporaneous ways of spectacle as well. In the following, I will start to explore how religion uses the spectacular ways of popular culture to convince young people of sexual abstinence until marriage. I will concentrate on the phenomenon of public virginity pledges. Although at first glance it seems that virginity pledges are a person's private matters and would go against a popular culture that is depicted by images of (graphic) sexuality, Christian chastity organizations are marked by their high visibility and their usage of spectacular popular culture techniques. However, virginity pledgers are not simply part of the dominant culture but form a specific "identity movement" that "provides a frame for self-understanding (and consequently action in pursuit of that understanding)" (Bearman and Brückner 870). The chastity movement creates a "moral community" in which pledgers participate and "take on a pledge identity" (Bearman and Brückner 900).

I will demonstrate here how this "identity movement" and "moral community" functions through the use of popular culture, the ascription of specific moral values, the representation of nonpledgers as "the others," and the suggestion of specific gender roles. First, I will sketch the general background of the virginity pledge movement and its development, as well as the reasons for the effectiveness of its program. In the second part, I will analyze the organization, *The Silver Ring Thing* (silverringthing.com). The last part of my paper will summarize the strategies of the movement and point towards some of their unexpected effects.

The History and Effectiveness of the Virginity Pledge Organizations

The virginity pledge movement (or abstinence movement) developed in the early 1990s as part of the Christian Sex Education Project. It was a project designed and overseen by adults for teenagers to reduce teenage pregnancy and spread moral values (Mehren 1). On January 13, 1993, the first "True Love Waits" team held its first meeting in Nashville, Tennessee ("TWL History"). "True Love Waits" was the first virginity pledge organization and became visible through its various public appearances. The "True Love Waits" community expects its members to deliver a public pledge in which they confirm that they will stay sexually abstinent until marriage. However, the organization's concept of chastity is not limited to sexual intercourse, but also forbids oral and anal sex, sexual touching, intimate relationships, and pornography ("FAQ About TLW").

Next to "True Love Waits," there are several other virginity pledge programs in the United States. One of the "fastest growing teen abstinence program[s]" ("The History") is "The Silver Ring Thing" which will be analyzed in the next part of this paper. It was established in 1996 by Denny and Amy Pattyn, who also reacted to the increasing number of teenage pregnancies in their area. It was started in Yuma, Arizona, but was moved to Pittsburgh, PA after four years ("The History"). The founders point out that

[t]he Silver Ring Thing leadership recognize[d] that the distribution of condoms or the practice of 'safer-sex' [would] not ensure protection from the physical, emotional and spiritual problems resulting from sexual activity among teens. The only way to reverse the moral decay of any youth culture [was] to inspire a change in the conduct and behavior from those within the culture. ("The History")

To promote the concept of sexual abstinence and reach their target group – middle and high school students at the ages of 12 to 18 – "The Silver Ring Thing" uses two means. The first is a high-tech mass live event, while the second one is a specific program for young people, called somewhat mysteriously the "SRT 434 Program." "SRT" stands for "Silver Ring Thing," "434" is an appropriate reference to the Bible, 1 Thess. 4.3-4: "God wants you to be holy, so you should keep clear of all sexual sin. Then each of you will control your body and live in holiness and honor." The program is held on a local level in various cities. To increase the program's effectiveness, it also involves the teens' parents and thus starts with a forty – minute parent seminar to inform the pledgers' parents about the program and their role in it ("Silver Ring Thing for Parents").

Since 1993, over 2.5 million young people have been involved in one of the various programs of the virginity pledge movement (Bearman and Brückner 1). However, academic research about the movement is rather limited and focuses first and foremost on the effectiveness of the abstinence programs. In "A Report of the Heritage Center for Data Analysis" entitled "Teens Who Make Virginity Pledges Have Substantially Improved Life Outcomes" by the conservative Heritage Foundation, Robert Rector, Kirk Johnson, and Jennifer Marshall claim to have found out that virginity pledgers have less premarital pregnancies, less health risks, and less sexual activities (1). They report that the general behavior of pledgers were much better than the one of nonpledgers (14). These claims are contradicted by Cynthia Dailard from the nondenominational American Psychological Society (APS) who found out that over 60% of the pupils who pledged to stay sexually abstinent until marriage during middle or high school broke their commitment in 2003 alone (5). Dailard continues to point out that although pledgers stated to have had less vaginal intercourse than nonpledgers, 55% of college student pledgers admitted to having had oral or anal sex, and she underlines that there was no proof of the effectiveness of any virginity pledge program (5-6).

If the abstinence programs do not work, why then did over 2.5 million young people join that movement? What makes the programs so attractive to adolescents? In the following part, I will examine the virginity pledge organization "The Silver Ring Thing" in order to understand the popularity and appeal of such programs.

"The Silver Ring Thing"

As already argued in the beginning of this paper, the virginity pledge movement is an "identity movement." It provides its members an "identity and fellowship with other pledgers" (Bearman and Brückner 870). Bearman and Brückner argue that the "pledge identity is induced and sustained through interacting with other pledgers in the community who distinguish themselves from nonpledgers by their public pledge and their commitment to the group" (870). Consequently, the self of the pledger is produced through its distinction from the self of the nonpledger (870).

The abstinence program "The Silver Ring Thing" provides its members with a new distinguished identity. This identity is marked by its high visibility and induced through several mechanisms: First, "the Silver Ring Thing" distinguishes itself from dominant secular popular culture through the rejection of a number of its values. In a letter to parents and sponsors the organization points out that there is "no question that the pressure and influence coming from TV, magazines, movies, the internet, and other media [have] destructively changed today's youth culture" ("SRT Ring Sponsorship"). However, instead of rejecting popular culture entirely, the organization uses a cleaned up, sanitized version for its own purposes. To recruit new members, "The Silver Ring Thing" uses high-tech equipment, loud pop music with Christian lyrics, special effects, neon lights, and fast changing images on large video screens in their 2 1/2 hour live stage performance events that are more reminiscent of MTV than of traditional venues to promote moral values like sexual abstinence. "The Silver Ring Thing" organizers explain this contradiction with the remark that in order to draw young people's attention to them, they have to use similar and sometimes even better technical equipment and performance styles than the ones used in secular popular culture ("Q&A"). In "Shake, Rattle & Roll. Production and Consumption of Fundamentalist Youth Culture," Heather Hendershot points out that through the use of popular culture, the "reassuring message directed at fundamentalist youth is that their religion does not marginalize them from the cultural mainstream" (*Afterimages*). Thus, on the one hand, "The Silver Ring Thing" uses popular culture as a means to reach young people and create a space in which they feel comfortable but, on the other hand, it discredits secular popular culture, because it is loaded with sexual content and sends the 'wrong' message.

"The Silver Ring Thing" uses popular American icons to instill their message of sexual abstinence. In 2003, the abstinence organization went on a small tour to different high and middle schools featuring the former Miss America, Erika Harold, to tell students how important it is to stay pure until marriage ("Media Coverage"). Harold's appearance on the abstinence program provided the movement with a positive, pretty, if not glamorous image. The pledger's identity is positively confirmed when a former Miss America announces publicly that she is one of them. Her popularity, her beauty, and fame rubs off onto the pledger community.

To create an identity that young pledgers would feel comfortable with, "The Silver Ring Thing" employs the language of today's youth. A promotion for a "Wild West Mission Trip" that "The Silver Ring Thing" organizes for young pledgers starts with the words "Ok crazy kids ... who wants to have a TOTAL BLAST this summer with SRT MI CREW? You better have all said 'HECK YES!'" ("Wild West Mission"). The capitalizing of words and phrases does not only underline them but mimes spoken, spontaneous language and is meant to transmit the excitement and fun that is announced in the ad's text. The abbreviations address the reader as part of a group

106

with a special identity, marked by language understood only by insiders. The exclamation marks, ellipses, and use of direct speech emphasize the sentences' dynamics
and are meant to produce the effect of youth street talk. Thus, the use of modern,
supposedly adolescent language fashions a young and dynamic image of the virginity
pledge organization.

To emphasize the pledger's newly chosen identity, "The Silver Ring Thing" offers various merchandise to secure the pledger's visibility. There are pledge books,
buttons, head gear, program packages, key chains, mugs, stickers, and T-shirts. Next
to the general program package, there is also an exclusive leather package available
for those members who want to distinguish themselves among their peers. The act
of consuming is encouraged, as in any other U.S. advertising campaign, through special offers. The invitation "Order any Eight Buttons for 5$," for instance, indicates
that the more one buys, the cheaper it will get ("Merchandise"). The buttons come in
bright colors and bear familiar but slightly modified images that transmit morally en-
hanced messages: one button displays a red skull in front of a black background with
the words "Safe Sex? Warning: No Condom Can Protect 100% Against Pregnancy,
AIDS, or any STD." A pedestrian sign depicts a man and a woman holding hands and
the words "We're Waiting," while a white road sign with a red circle informs "Warning: Sex Chances Everything." Another road sign is inscribed with the words "Don't
Drink & Park. Accidents Cause Kids." And instead of displaying the well-known at-
tractions of a Hard Rock Café, one button uses its image to promote the abstinence
program by replacing "Hard Rock Café" with the words "Silver Ring Thing." Thus,
the buttons take up common popular images and add rather humorous texts as well as
warning messages.

The most important material item is the silver ring that each pledger can purchase
for $20 after his or her commitment to sexual abstinence. The purpose of the ring
is to display it on one's finger until one's wedding day, in order to exchange it for
a wedding ring. The ring serves as a visible symbol or marker of the identity of the
virginity pledger, yet it is just an outward sign of inner values. "The Silver Ring Thing"
organization stresses on its webpage that "the ring is not a 'piece of jewelry'" and that
it is "worn as the symbol and constant reminder of the faith decision and vow pledged
to God Almighty" ("Ring Care").

The identity ascribed to the pledgers is clearly streamlined according to two gen-
ders. The merchandise section, for example, offers "Shirts for Girls" and plain "T-
Shirts." The shirts for girls are mainly pink and tight, and thus emphasize the physical
otherness of young women. The shirts bear flowers as, for instance, the "Asian Girl
Shirt," and hearts, on the so-called "Heart Girl Shirt." The form and color of the or-
naments connote sweetness, closeness to nature, and loveliness. In comparison, the
general T-shirt section is not entitled "Shirts for Boys," the counterpart of "Shirts for
Girls," although it obviously is meant to offer only male clothing. Consequently, the

movement's shirt labels already represent girls as the "other," the ab-normal, who are marked by the deviation from a male norm. This hints towards an assumed natural, yet strictly hierarchical order of boys as the norm, therefore the superior, and girls as deviations, therefore the inferior sex. The naturalized differences between girls and boys is also underlined by the choice of color of the T-shirts, which supplies – not surprisingly – girls with mostly pink and red, boys with black, blue, and brown shirts.

So far, I have explained why the pledge movement is an identity movement. I will now demonstrate why it can also be understood as a "moral community" (Bearman and Brückner 900). A "moral community" can only exist as long as there is another part of culture to whom the community is morally superior. This means that the pledge movement has to represent all nonpledgers as "others;" "other" because they are not able to reach the moral community's moral standards. This again can be demonstrated on the basis of the merchandise samples, which actively participate in the "othering" of nonmembers. One of the shirts for girls, for instance, bears the words "good girl" ("Merchandise"). The "goodness" of the girl refers, of course, to her commitment of sexual abstinence. However, if staying abstinent is considered good, all girls having not abstained before marriage are stigmatized as "bad girls." [This is problematic, even if one agrees that young girls should not be sexually active, because the "bad girls" would also include girls who were raped, and thus could not stay virgins until marriage.] One of the merchandise buttons states, "We're waiting." The "We" is again used as a counterpart to an implicit "other," a "You" that is not waiting, and therefore not behaving in a morally appropriate way. Another button reads "Warning: Sex Changes Everything," and thus represents its wearer paradoxically as an expert on questions concerning sexual activity, although he or she has not had sexual experiences yet. The words on the button suggest that sexual intercourse is something scary, and that people should beware of it.

To emphasize that the organization disagrees with the morals of the secular culture, "The Silver Ring Thing," on its webpage, offers not only a free porn filter for the internet, but also illustrates the dangers of sexual intercourse in the form of statistics. The statistics give the amount of people infected by STDs (sexual transmitted diseases), with specific focus on AIDS. However, there are no specifics or background information given, neither on the statistics nor on the diseases which, as for instance in the case of AIDS, may not only be contracted through sexual intercourse. The figures are obviously instrumentalized to spread fear among, and scare young people not to leave the "moral community" and at the same time to chastise and "other" the ones who do not belong to it.

This "moral community" promotes the involvement of parents. It encourages mothers and fathers to join the program's activities and events, and provides them with additional parent packages to support their sons and daughters. However, there are parents who do not agree with their children's decision to be a part of an abstinence program and they are thoroughly "othered," too. "The Silver Ring Thing" organization points out that they do "recognize that not every student is fortunate to have a supportive parent who is involved in his or her life," so that for "these kids, the SRT follow-up program, with one-on-one mentoring and peer group support offers an essential alternative parental support" ("Q&A"). Thereby, "The Silver Ring Thing" puts itself above the authority of pledgers' parents who do not go along with SRT-values, and judges nonpledge supporting parents as non-supportive parents who function as "the other," and are thus inferior. These "inferior" parents are substituted by a morally superior, "essential alternative paren[t]" of "The Silver Ring Thing" program.

The morals instilled by the community are obviously not always easy to keep. One of the biggest sections of "The Silver Ring Thing" webpage is dedicated to "Devotionals" in which young people tell about their personal experiences with the program, and offer advice in how to avoid the trappings of sexual activity. In an essay entitled "How Far is Too Far?" pledgers are reminded to keep their commitment in order to not deceive themselves and their future wives or husbands. In "More Reasons to Wait," the pledgers are promised to be rewarded by God's "amazing blessings when [they] do things His way and wait until [they are] married" ("Devotional #4"). A young soldier who went to Iraq states on the "Silver Ring Thing" webpage that even "out there in the desert where you least expect it the enemy is waiting to catch you off guard [sic], but I still stand firm" ("Devotional #2"). If "the enemy" refers to the sinful world that the soldier is no longer part of, to the Iraqi people in general, or to certain individuals in particular, is not clear. However, the young soldier constructs himself as the moral "I" who stands "firm" against the evil "other."

Conclusion

On account of the preceding analysis, it became clear that the virginity pledge organization "The Silver Ring Thing" is so popular, because it is constructed as a "moral community" (Bearman and Brückner 900). It offers communal support to people in a complicated and potentially alienating and confusing period of life. It understands itself as morally superior to the dominant culture, rejects nonpledgers as the "others," and acts as an authority on questions concerning sexuality. By using the binary opposition of moral goodness versus moral badness, the program recruits young people by successfully using the time-honored method of "othering." The thinking in mutually exclusive oppositions is not only a constant in Christian fundamentalist discourses, but has also often been used in U.S. politics (in the 1950s, it was directed against "Communists," and today it is used against "terrorists"). Thus, the technique of community creation by "othering" is something Americans are well familiar with.

As shown in my analysis, "The Silver Ring Thing" also became so popular among young people in the United States, because it is constructed as an "identity movement" that speaks the language of the youth and employs popular culture. The consumption of virginity pledge products that are represented as "cool commodities [. . .] make kids feel less alienated from American consumer culture" (Hendershot, *Shaking* 34). Thus, the young pledgers participate in and are part of consumer culture. However, the abstinence movement is not part of dominant culture. Although "The Silver Ring Thing" uses the spectacles of mainstream popular culture, its content is different. Thus, "The Silver Ring Thing" sends a religious message wrapped up in a secular envelope.

However, the organization's secular envelope works not only on the level of popular representation and ideology, but also on the political and financial level. Starting under the Ronald Reagan administration in 1981, the U.S. Government had been funding abstinence-only-until-marriage programs until Barack Obama took office in 2009. Especially under George W. Bush, the executive branch promoted pro-abstinence discourses as demonstrated by Claire Greslé-Favier in *"Raising Sexually Pure Kids": Sexual Abstinence, Conservative Christians and American Politics.* If the money had been spent on religious organizations, the governmental funding of pro-abstinence programs would not have been possible. Yet, as the programs were propagated as politically and religiously neutral, there was no hindrance to their financial support. Between 1996 and 2006 alone, Congress and state governments spent $1.5 billion to support abstinence organizations ("A Brief History"). For further research it would be interesting to have a closer look at these veiled interconnections between state and religious movement in a country which prides itself in its complete division between church and state.

Works Cited

"A Brief History of Abstinence-Only-Until-Marriage Funding." *NoNewMoney.* SIECUS. 2005. Web. 10 Jul. 2007.

Bearman, Peter S. and Hannah Brückner. "Promising the Future. Virginity Pledges and First Intercourse." *American Journal of Sociology* 106.4 (2001): 859-912. Print.

Carbett, Julia Mitchell. *Religion in America.* Upper Saddle River: Prentice Hall, 2000. Print.

Dailard, Cynthia. "Understanding 'Abstinence.' Implications for Individuals, Programs and Policies." *The Guttmacher Report on Public Policy.* Vol. 4 (Dec. 2003): 4-6. Print.

Debord, Guy. *Comments on the Society of the Spectacle.* London: Biddles, 1990. Print.

Silverringthing. Silver Ring Thing. N.d. Web. 29 Apr. 2007.

"FAQ About TLW For Youth." *LifeWay Christian Resources.* LifeWay: Biblical Solutions for Life. 2001-2007. Web. 25 Apr. 2007.

Forbes, Bruce David. "Introduction. Finding Religion in Unexpected Places." *Religion and Popular Culture in America.* Bruce David Forbes and Jeffrey H. Mahan. Berkeley: U of California P, 2005. Print.

Greslé-Favier, Claire. *'Raising Sexually Pure Kids': Sexual Abstinence, Conservative Christians and American Politics.* Rodopi: New York, 2009.

Hendershot, Heather. "Shake, Rattle & Roll. Production and Consumption of Fundamentalist Youth Culture." *Afterimages.* N.p. Feb./Mar. 1995. Web. 29 Apr. 2007.

—. *Shaking the World for Jesus. Media and Conservative Evangelical Culture.* Chicago: U of Chicago P, 2004. Print.

—. "Virgins for Jesus. The Gender Politics of Therapeutic Christian Fundamentalist Media." *Hop on Pop. The Politics and Pleasures of Popular Culture.* Eds. Henry Jenkin, Tara McPherson, and Jane Shattuc. Durham: Duke UP, 2002. Print.

Mehren, Elizabeth. "Some may play fast and loose with virginity pledge, study finds." *San Francisco Chronicle* May 8 (2006): A-2. Print.

Peters, Ulrike. *Grosses Wörterbuch Religion. Grundwissen von A-Z.* München 2008.

Rector, Robert, Kirk Johnson and Jennifer Marshall. "Teens Who Make Virginity Pledges Have Substantially Improved Life Outcomes." *A Report of the Heritage Center for Data Analysis* Sept. 21 (2004): 1-15. Print.

"TWL History." *LifeWay Christian Resources.* LifeWay: Biblical Solutions for Life. 2001–2007. Web. 25 Apr. 2007.

Contributors

Gunnar Berndt is currently the Communications Manager with the Los Angeles Blues professional soccer team in Santa Monica, California. He also runs his own linguistic services agency, *lingualutions*, based out of Düsseldorf, Germany.

Petra Danielczyk holds an M.A. in English and Educational Science from Ruhr-University Bochum. Her major areas of research are American literature and English literature before 1700, with a focus on gender studies, ecotopias and American consumer culture. She recently taught German at the University of South Carolina.

Elisa Edwards is currently working in the American Studies department at Ruhr-University Bochum. Her major areas of research are images of Germany in American literature, African American Studies, and Cultural Studies. She has recently published *Race, Aliens, and the U.S. Government in African American Science Fiction* (2011).

Kornelia Freitag is the Chair of American Studies at Ruhr-University Bochum. Her major areas of research are cultural and literary theory, contemporary American poetry, and ethnic literature. She has recently co-edited together with Jeanne Cortiel, Christine Gerhardt, and Michael Wala *Religion in the United States* (2010).

Daniel Timothy Goering studied History and American Studies at Yale University and Ruhr-University Bochum and is currently a PhD candidate in the History Department at Ruhr-University Bochum. In his doctoral thesis he is focusing on the shifting role of religion in the German public sphere during the 20th century. His research interests include Modern Religious History and Modern European Intellectual History.

Cornelius Herz is currently working as a preparatory school teacher in Bochum. His research interests include teaching methodology and the historical constructions of authorship, copyright, as well as the notion of "literature." He is writing his PhD thesis on the teaching of media upheavals.

Raphaela Holinski holds a B.A. (2007) and an M.Ed. (2009) in English and American Studies and Protestant Theology from Ruhr-University Bochum and an

M.A. in Modern Literary Studies (2008) from Queen's University Belfast. She is currently completing her PhD on Ireland's involvement in the 1857 Indian 'Mutiny' at Queen's University Belfast. Her main research interests lie in the area of nineteenth-century British literary and cultural studies.

Christian Lenz is a research assistant at TU Dortmund at the department of British Cultural Studies. He is currently completing his PhD on spatial notions and compatibilities in chick- and ladlit. His research foci are on cultural geography, contemporary British literature and film as well as on horror, with special emphasis on zombies.

Moritz Schuster is teaching English and Social Sciences at Max-Planck-Gymnasium Gelsenkirchen. He focuses on teaching parliament simulations and currently writes a teacher's guide to the Model European Parliament. He plays drums in the Hard Rock/Metal outfit Layment, who celebrate their 15th anniversary and are about to release their third studio album.

Maria Verena Siebert is working on her PhD thesis on crossover literature and the kidult consumer on the example of *Harry Potter* and *Twilight*. Her major research interests are media and gender studies. She is currently teaching Cultural Studies in Bochum and Göttingen.